I0410379

USDA

United States
Department of
Agriculture

Forest Service

**Northern
Research Station**

General Technical
Report NRS-11

Managing Timber to Promote Sustainable Forests: A Second-Level Course for the Sustainable Forestry Initiative of Pennsylvania

James C. Finley
Susan L. Stout
Timothy G. Pierson
Barbara J. McGuinness

Abstract

At least 80 percent of the raw material used for wood products by the forest industry is from privately owned woodlands. This publication provides material for a course designed to help landowners, foresters, and loggers work together to assess whether a planned timber harvest will retain the diversity of species on site. It includes methods for collecting overstory and understory data, inspecting these data, and assessing sustainability.

The Authors

JAMES C. FINLEY is a professor with Pennsylvania State University, School of Forest Resources, University Park, Pennsylvania.

SUSAN L. STOUT is a research forester and Project Leader with the Northern Research Station's Forestry Sciences Laboratory at Warren, Pennsylvania.

TIMOTHY G. PIERSON is a cooperative extension forester and educator with Pennsylvania State University, University Park, Pennsylvania.

BARBARA J MCGUINNESS is a forester with the Northern Research Station's Forestry Sciences Laboratory at Warren, Pennsylvania.

Manuscript received for publication 7 August 2006

Acknowledgment

The materials in this book were developed through a partnership among the USDA Forest Service Northern Research Station, the Pennsylvania State University, and the Pennsylvania Sustainable Forestry Initiative Program State Implementation committee (SFI SIC). The SFI SIC will use them in training programs for timber harvesters and landowners. Individuals interested in sustainable forestry also will find them valuable for self-study and application.

PENNSTATE

College of Agricultural Sciences

CONTENTS

Introduction 1

Assessment Procedures 3

   Laying Out Your Survey 3

   Regeneration Assessment Procedure 4

      Field Measurements 4

      Regeneration Assessment Variables 5

Overstory Assessment Procedure 8

      Field Measurements 9

   Setting Up the Tally Sheet 9

   Collecting Overstory Data 9

Field Data Summary 13

   Summarizing Regeneration Data 13

      Deer Impact 13

      Advanced Regeneration 13

      Canopy Density 13

      Interference 13

   Summarizing Overstory Data 14

      Species Composition 14

      Seed Source 15

      Residual Tree Quality 17

      Average Stand Diameter 18

   Interpreting the Overstory Assessment Tally Sheet 22

      The Sustainability Key 22

      Alternative Treatment 24

What Have We Learned? 27

Additional Resources 27

Appendix A Estimating Average Stand Diameter 28

Appendix B Understory and Overstory Tally Sheets 30

Appendix C Timber Harvesting Assessment and Treatment Unit Sustainability
   Assessment Forms 32

Forest Stewardship Bulletin No. 12 34

INTRODUCTION

Sustainable forestry includes caring for wildlife, protecting water, providing recreation, and sustaining timber resources. The Sustainable Forestry Initiative (SFI) is built around core guiding principles that call upon participants to "meet market demands while using environmentally responsible practices that promote the protection of wildlife, plants, soil, and air and water quality." Another guiding principle of SFI is to "meet the needs of the present without compromising the ability of future generations to meet their own needs by practicing a land stewardship ethic."

Other continuing education courses through SFI of Pennsylvania cover introductions to forest ecology and silviculture, the importance of determining landowner objectives, effects of logging on wildlife habitat, road layout, and Best Management Practices (BMPs). This course focuses on timber resources, specifically, on assessing whether a planned timber harvest will retain timber species on the site. You will learn how to take regeneration and overstory data in the field, interpret the data, and use a key to assess whether or not a harvest sustains desired species diversity.

Private forest-land owners contribute at least 80 percent or more of the raw material used by the forest industry to make a myriad of wood products. Certainly, landowners have a responsibility to make the right decisions to achieve sustainable outcomes, but they depend on all of us—timber harvesters, foresters, and the forest products industry—to guide them toward making responsible forestry decisions. We are all responsible for promoting good forestry and protecting forest resources for future generations (Fig. 1).

Retaining timber species onsite allows us to maintain the potential of the future forest.

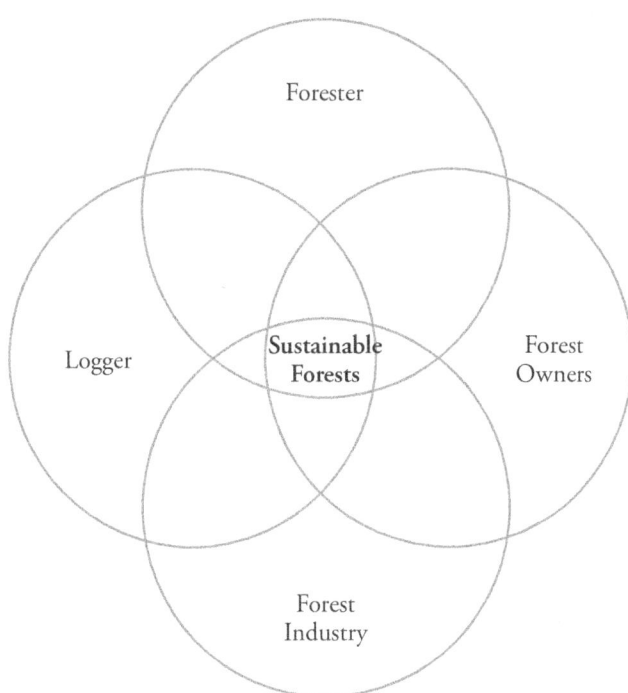

Figure 1.—Sustainability is everyone's responsibility.

Silviculture is the art and science of controlling the establishment, growth, composition, health, and quality of forests and woodlands to meet the diverse needs and values of landowners and society on a sustainable basis.

Traditionally, a forester would apply silviculture to develop a prescription designed to obtain a sustainable, healthy future forest, and a timber harvester would provide the expertise necessary for implementing a harvest, taking care to protect the soil resource and residual trees. However, many timber harvests in Pennsylvania are direct transactions between the timber harvester and the landowner. The assessment tool provided in this course will help timber harvesters and landowners apply basic principles of silviculture to promote sustainable forestry outcomes.

We will consider eight questions that focus our attention on existing and potential regeneration on the site, and the trees that will remain after the harvest (residual trees).

Regeneration:

- What is the impact of white-tailed deer?
- What is the condition of the existing advanced regeneration?
- How will light affect existing and potential regeneration?
- What is the role of interfering plants?

Residual trees:

- What will happen to species composition?
- Will adequate seed source be retained?
- What will happen to residual tree quality?
- What will happen to the average stand diameter?

Throughout this document, sidebars with shaded trees are used for definitions and discussion of the sample stand. Sidebars in boxes display threshold levels for sustainable forestry.

ASSESSMENT PROCEDURES
Laying Out Your Survey

Before you collect data, walk through the area that you plan to harvest and consider the size of the area and the variability in both the overstory and understory vegetation. This exercise will help you determine how many plots to take and where to collect data within the area.

If the area is large and there is variation in the vegetation, consider dividing the entire harvest area into subunits of similar conditions (called stands), and making a separate assessment in each subunit. For example, if there are noticeable differences in the vegetation (one area has a high proportion of oak and a carpet of small oak seedlings, another has a high proportion of beech/hemlock and scarce regeneration), these areas can be treated as separate stands.

Within each harvest unit, or within each individual stand, you must determine how many plots to take. Table 1 shows the minimum number of plots to take in harvest units of different size; taking more plots increases the reliability of results. Foresters usually take more plots to develop an accurate assessment of overstory and understory conditions to develop silvicultural prescriptions. Often, the number of understory plots is twice the number of overstory observations since understory conditions frequently are more variable than overstory conditions. Your confidence in the results of your survey and the accuracy of your information will increase as you increase the number of plots.

Stands are forested subunits that are uniform in species composition, tree size, age, site conditions, and history.

Where do you locate the plots? Again, consider the size and variability of the harvest unit. Choose a route through your harvest unit (you can double back in large areas) that allows you to establish the overstory and understory plots so that they are spaced fairly equally throughout the harvest unit. Make sure that the plot locations represent conditions throughout the area.

Try not to "choose" areas because they are easier to measure or because there are more trees there. If you do, the results will biased. Do not locate a plot so that it includes an existing road, forest edge, or any thing that makes the plot unique or does not represent the variation in the stand, for example, a plot on the same contour or on a bench.

Table 1.—Minimum number of plots for assessing stand and harvest area conditions (additional plots increase accuracy)

Harvest area (acres)	Minimum number of plots per harvest
25 or less	5
26-100	10
101-200	15
More than 200	20

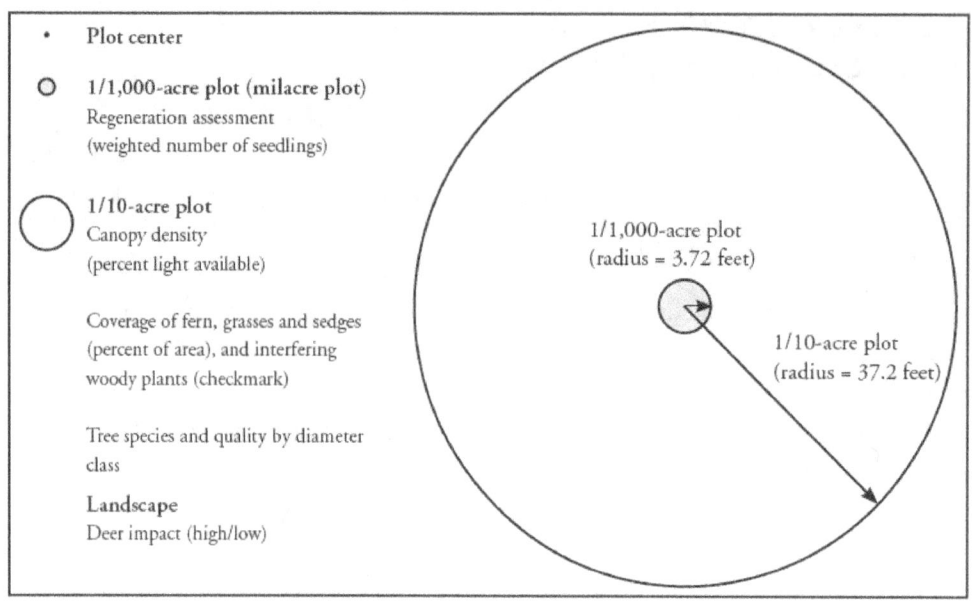

Figure 2.—Plot layout and data collected.

At each plot, use the same plot center for both the understory and overstory plots. Overstory measurements are taken on a 1/10-acre plot (a circular plot with a radius of 37.2 feet) and understory data are collected on both a 1/1,000-acre (milacre) plot (a circular plot with a radius of 3.72 feet) and the 1/10-acre plot.

The first few times you measure your plots, use a logger's tape or marked rope to measure the plot's limits. With practice, you will be able to assess this distance without measuring every time. However, it is useful to check yourself periodically, especially if you suspect that a tree is on the edge of the plot. Figure 2 shows how each combination overstory/understory plot is laid out.

Regeneration Assessment Procedure

Every harvest, even a light one, must consider the effect on understory conditions. Begin with the regeneration assessment at each plot. This portion of the assessment is intended to answer the following regeneration questions:

- What is the impact of white-tailed deer?
- What is the condition of the existing advanced regeneration?
- How will light affect existing and potential regeneration?
- What is the role of interfering plants?

Field Measurements

Recognizing the existence and abundance of advanced regeneration and the barriers posed by white-tailed deer and interfering plants are keys to assessing the sustainability of a planned harvest, especially if a large portion of the overstory will be removed. The intent is not to obtain exact values but to estimate values relative to thresholds in a decision tree. Figure 2 shows the measurements taken to assess regeneration potential.

Plot	1 Deer Impact (H/L)	2 Regen. Adequate	3 Canopy Density (percent)	4 Fern (percent)	5 Grasses/ sedges (percent)	6 Woody plants (percent)	7 Any Interference (check)
1		20	50	40	20	10	√
2		0	40	70	10	15	√
3		50+	40	40	0	5	√
4		50+	30	20	0	20	
5		10	40	30	20	10	√
		percent stocked	average percent	percent ≥ 30	percent ≥ 30	percent ≥ 30	percent with √
Stand	H						

Figure 3.—Example regeneration tally sheet for harvest area or stand of 25 acres or less.

Other items or variables can enter the decision but are more difficult to assess or are encountered less often. Among these are rocks, water, and poor soil drainage, as well as sprouting and potential seed production. The focus of the assessment in this course is to raise awareness about the condition of the stand before harvesting and its relationship to the condition of the stand following harvesting. Figure 3 is a sample tally sheet used to collect and summarize regeneration data.

Regeneration Assessment Variables

White-tailed deer. Across Pennsylvania, regeneration failures are common and deer along with other factors often are the cause. The effect of white-tailed deer on forest regeneration is extremely variable across the State and depends on current and historic population levels, alternative food sources, and cover. On the basis of the description of the impacts of white-tailed deer that follows, record an estimate of whether the effect of deer on regeneration success will be high (H) or low (L) in the harvest area as a whole. Look beyond your plot for this assessment; consider the impact of deer across the harvest area and even at the landscape level (one square mile or more).

Evidence of high deer impact is demonstrated by heavy browse damage on seedlings, understories that are dominated by species that deer avoid or that are resilient to deer browsing (see list at left), or high crop damage on local farmland. Harvest areas with a low deer impact will have diverse understory species that are variable in height and no visible browse line. Assessment of this variable should include discussions with adjacent landowners and observations of conditions on their properties.

Record deer impact for the entire harvest area. Checking with the local wildlife conservation officers or foresters for their assessment of the local situation is another useful way to estimate the deer density and probable impact. If the landowner is planning to fence the harvest area immediately following the timber harvest, mark the stand as low deer impact.

Species that dominate where deer density is high:

Herbaceous plants: ferns, grasses

Shrubs: blueberry, mountain laurel, sweet fern, spicebush

Woody species: beech, striped maple

Table 2.—Regeneration weights by seedling height

Weight	Seedling height
1	2 inches to 1 foot
2	1 foot to 3 feet
20	3 feet to 5 feet
50	5 feet and taller

Table 3.—Regeneration thresholds by deer impact (1/1,000-acre plot)

Deer impact	Weighted number of seedlings per milacre plot
Low	15
High	50

> **Forest regeneration threshold:**
>
> Deer impact affects forest regeneration thresholds. With high deer densities, it is necessary to have a weighted count of 50 seedlings per plot. Under low deer impact, the required weighted count is 15 seedlings per plot.

Forest regeneration. Forest regeneration is assessed on the 1/1,000-acre plot. The focus of this evaluation is on commercially desirable tree species. In Pennsylvania, most of the tree species in this category depend on seedlings established before harvest as the most reliable source of regeneration. Hence, the focus for this variable is on established (advanced) regeneration.

The condition of regeneration, especially its age and size, is an important consideration. Seedlings that are at least one growing season old are better than new germinants. Gently tug on several small seedlings. Those that pull from the soil or have roots only in the litter layer are less likely to survive or develop. Do not count them in the assessment. Give extra weight to larger and older seedlings (see Table 2) as they are more likely to survive. Record a weighted count of the seedlings of desirable species on your milacre regeneration plot. Estimate by multiples of 5 up to 50 seedlings; if you have more than 50 seedlings, record 50+.

Stump sprouts and seeds stored in the forest litter also are sources of regeneration. If you or the landowner wish to count on these sources, use a more sophisticated assessment tool. Where deer impact is high, more or larger seedlings are required. The values in Table 3 set minimum seedling densities per plot for adequate advanced regeneration.

As an example, 50 small seedlings (less than 1 foot tall) of desirable species on a plot are sufficient regeneration at low or high deer impact. Another plot with 25 small seedlings and 1 seedling 3 to 5 feet tall (counted as 20 in Table 2) has a total weighted count of 45 seedlings. This is insufficient regeneration for a plot in a high-deer-impact area, though the plot would meet the threshold as an area with low deer impact.

Canopy density. Light is a critical factor in evaluating the likelihood of regeneration. The amount of light striking the forest floor helps us evaluate the relative importance of

> **Canopy density threshold:**
>
> Canopy closure of less than 50 percent suggests a regeneration harvest.

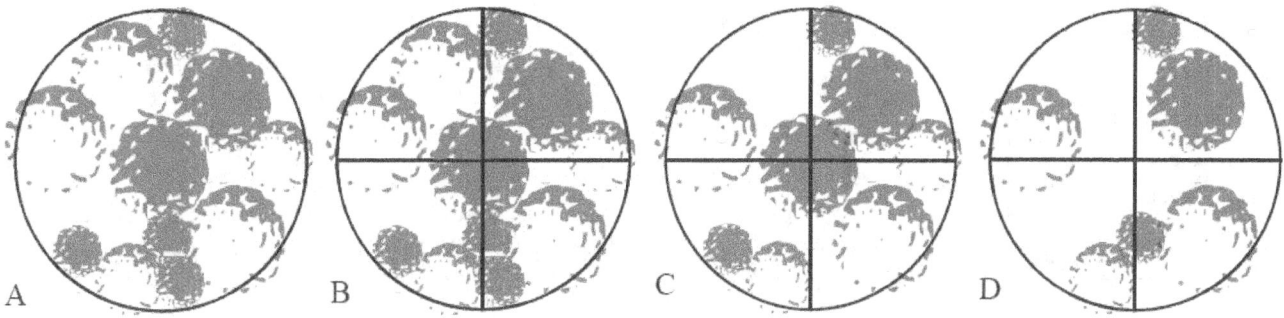

Figure 4.—**Estimating crown density on the 1/10-acre plot helps us consider the effect of light on the future stand.** Consider the preharvest crown closure (A). By mentally placing the crown coverage on a pie grid (B), we can estimate preharvest crown closure at 85 percent. A partial cut (C) may leave 60 percent, while a regeneration harvest (D) leaves less than 50-percent canopy closure.

residual trees or regeneration after the harvest, and whether to designate the harvest as a partial cut or a regeneration cut.

To measure canopy density you must look ahead to conditions that will exist after the harvest. Therefore, you have to decide which trees will remain and which will be cut. Looking straight up at several points in the 1/10-acre plot, record your average estimate of the percentage of sky (in increments of 10 percent) that will be filled by the forest canopy following the harvest (see Figure 4 for an example). This is an acquired skill and will take some time during your first several assessments. Record this estimate for every plot in the harvest area.

Ferns. Ferns interfere with seedling regeneration in several ways. Most importantly, they capture light that seeds require to sprout and seedlings need to grow. Record an estimate of the percentage of the ground (in increments of 10 percent) on the 1/10-acre plot that is completely shaded by single-frond ferns (see below). As with crown density, mentally "squeeze" dispersed fern cover into a patch with 100 percent cover, and estimate the percentage of the plot covered.

For this assessment, ferns fall into two categories: those that grow in clumps and those with single fronds or leaves. Among the clump ferns are Christmas, interrupted, sword, and woods ferns. These dot the landscape, forming obvious clumps. They spread slowly and rarely form dense, continuous shade across large expanses of forest area.

The single-frond ferns can spread rapidly. Among those this group of special concern are New York, hayscented, and bracken ferns. The first two have single, heavily divided leaves that originate from aggressive underground rhizomes. Bracken fern has a single stem that rises 2 feet or more above the forest floor before dividing into three fronds or leaves.

For all practical purposes, deer do not eat ferns. Hence, because of historically high white-tailed deer populations, fern occurrence and density is on the increase. Disturbance from logging leads to increased light levels and encourages ferns to spread.

Fern threshold:

When 30 percent or more of an area is covered by fern, it is likely to interfere with the establishment and development of regeneration after a partial cut.

Grasses and sedges. Grasses and sedges interfere with tree establishment in much the same way as ferns. Dense grasses and sedges cause shade, inhibiting the development of tree seedlings. When considering these plants, focus on the amount of shade they produce. As with ferns, visually "squeeze" all the grass and sedge into a clump and estimate the percentage of the plot it covers. Record the percentage of the plot area in increments of 10 percent. If there are even trace amounts of grass or sedge, record 1 percent or 5 percent. These traces indicate a seedbank and should influence the choice of herbicide if such a treatment is planned.

Sedges are grassy plants with wedge-shaped leaves. Most sedges have triangular stems when viewed in cross section and their leaves grow on all three sides of the stems. Sedge stems also are solid. Grass stems often are round and always are hollow. Grass leaves grow on two sides of the stalk. Sedges can indicate seasonally wet soils. Removing too much of the overstory may increase soil moisture, encouraging aggressive sedge expansion and creating difficult conditions for seedling establishment and growth. If you observe that many of the plants recorded on your plot are sedges and the planned cut is heavy, draw the landowner's attention to the risk of exacerbating a soil-moisture problem.

Woody plants. Some woody plants can develop as dense canopies (up to 30 feet tall) under the overstory, interfering with establishing adequate regeneration through the shade they cast,. Some of the recognized species of concern are primarily shade-tolerant species like mountain laurel, ironwood (hophornbeam), musclewood (hornbeam), striped maple, black birch, sweet fern, blueberries, and beech. Some of these plants provide food or cover for wildlife and enhance species diversity. They can prevent regeneration however, when they dominate the forest understory. Record your estimate of the percentage of the 1/10-acre plot that is covered by the shade cast by these plants. Focus your estimate from ground level up to 30 feet.

Any interference. This variable captures the presence or absence of interference on a plot. We assess each interfering plant separately and then record a checkmark in this column if any species meets or exceeds the 30-percent threshold. If any cover for ferns, grasses and sedges, or woody plants is equal to or greater than 30 percent, record a checkmark in this column.

Overstory Assessment Procedure

This portion of the assessment is designed to answer the following residual tree questions:

- What will happen to species composition?
- Will the seed source be retained?
- What will happen to residual tree quality?
- What will happen to the average stand diameter?

Field Measurements

Controlling timber species composition, seed source, residual stem quality, and diameter distribution is the key to attaining a sustainable harvest. By using the procedures that follow, you will develop a picture of the stand before harvesting that will suggest whether the intended harvest will be sustainable.

Setting Up the Tally Sheet

The larger top part of the overstory assessment tally sheet in Figure 5 works from the bottom up. The size class line defines four diameter classes: 3 to 5.5 inches, 5.6 to 11.5 inches, 11.6 to 17.5 inches, and 17.6 inches and larger. List the species that occur for each diameter class and enter the species code. Start in the left-hand column of a given diameter class and list the shade-tolerant species followed by intermediates and finally the intolerants.

In northern hardwood forests, typical shade-tolerant species include sugar maple (HM), hemlock (HE), and American beech (BE). Intermediates include red maple (RM), red oak (RO), white oak (WO), black oak (BO), chestnut oak (CO), other oaks (OO), hickory (HI), white ash (WA), yellow birch (YB), black birch (BB), and black gum (BG). Intolerant species include white pine (WP), black cherry (BC), yellow-poplar, (YP), cucumbertree (CU), Virginia pine (VP), and aspen (AS).

In our example stand (Figure 6), species would be listed in the following order from left to right: HE, SM, RO, WO, YP, and BC. This provides a view of size classes by species and tolerance. This requires practice but by doing it you will develop insights into how harvesting affects species composition and stand structure.

Collecting Overstory Data

On the overstory tally sheet, record all trees larger than 3 inches on your first 1/10-acre plot. You need not mark individual trees but remember which tree was first and go around the plot in a clockwise or counterclockwise direction. Be consistent so that you do not miss a tree or count a tree twice.

For each tree encountered, measure its diameter at breast height (d.b.h.), which is measured at 4.5 feet above the ground. Because we are using diameter classes, eventually you will be able to estimate the size class for most trees. When in doubt, always measure the tree. Using the d.b.h., record the tree in one of the four diameter classes in the correct species column.

Record the tree using a symbol for its tree-condition code. Acceptable growing stock (AGS) contains or potentially contains at least one sawlog and will survive until the next harvest (record with a "+"). Unacceptable growing stock (UGS) never will produce a sawlog or is likely to die before the next harvest (record with a "-"). If you plan to harvest the tree, circle the quality code. The completed tally sheet for one plot will look something like Figure 7.

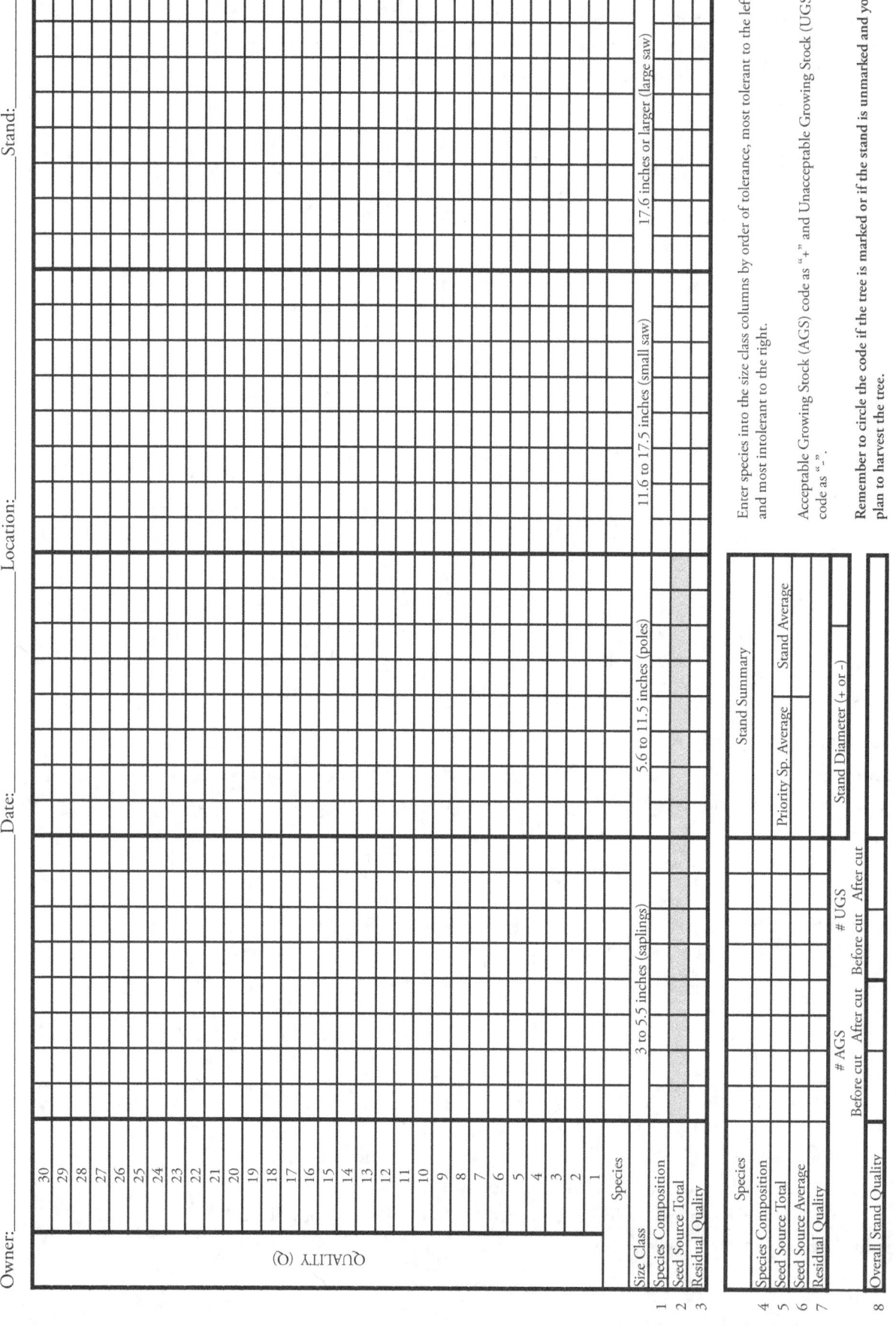

Figure 5.—Overstory assessment tally sheet.

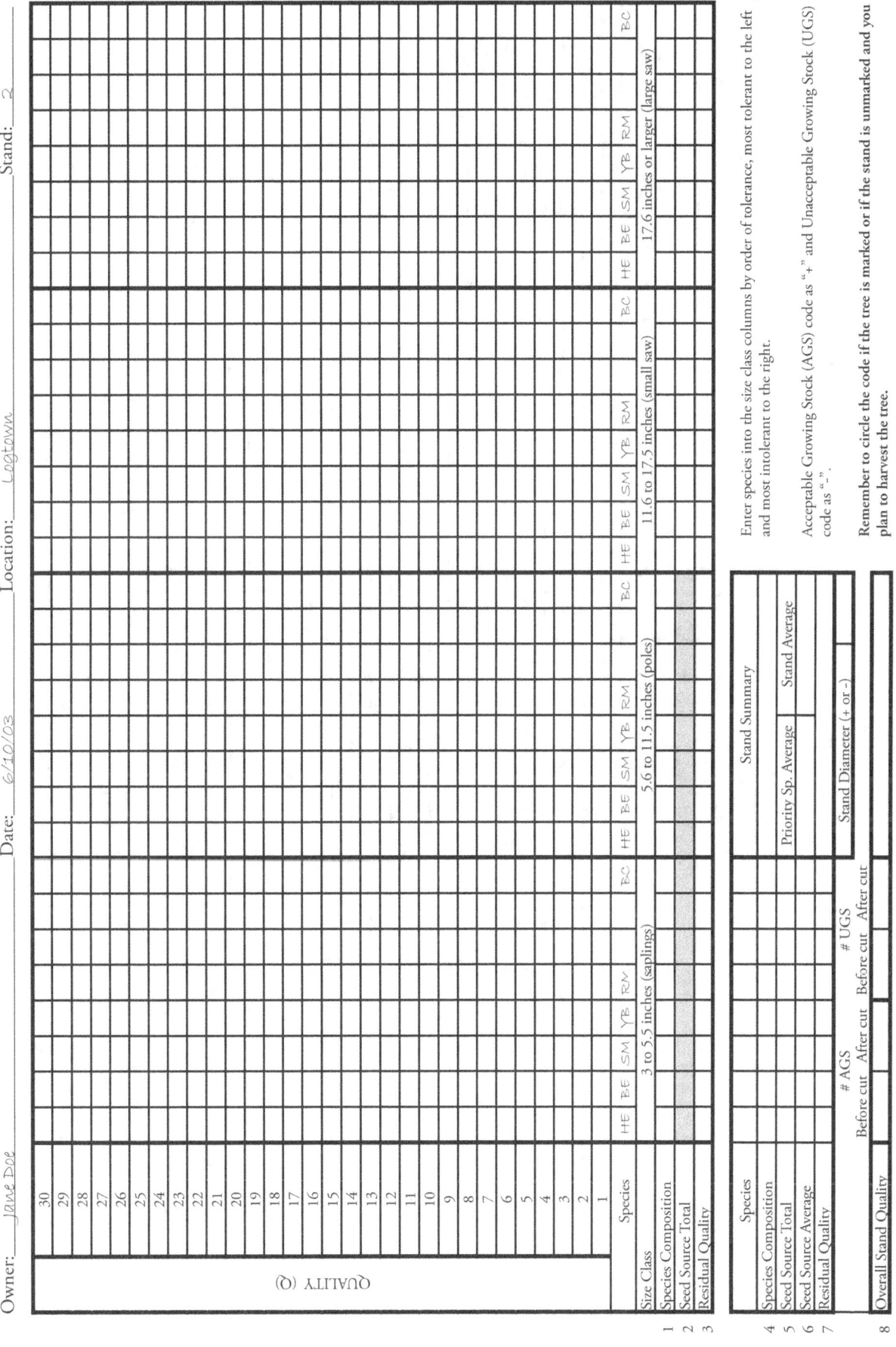

Figure 6.—Overstory assessment tally sheet with species codes.

Owner: _Jane Doe_   Date: _6/10/03_   Location: _Logtown_   Stand: _2_

QUALITY (Q)

Columns numbered 30 down to 1.

Species	HE BE SM YB RM	BC	HE BE SM YB RM	BC	HE BE SM YB RM	BC	HE BE SM YB RM	BC
1 Species Composition								
2 Seed Source Total								
3 Residual Quality								

Size Class	3 to 5.5 inches (saplings)	5.6 to 11.5 inches (poles)	11.6 to 17.5 inches (small saw)	17.6 inches or larger (large saw)

Stand Summary

Species	Priority Sp. Average	Stand Average
4 Species Composition		
5 Seed Source Total		
6 Seed Source Average		
7 Residual Quality		

Stand Diameter (+ or -)

	#AGS		#UGS	
	Before cut	After cut	Before cut	After cut

8 Overall Stand Quality

Enter species into the size class columns by order of tolerance, most tolerant to the left and most intolerant to the right.

Acceptable Growing Stock (AGS) code as " + " and Unacceptable Growing Stock (UGS) code as " - ".

Remember to circle the code if the tree is marked or if the stand is unmarked and you plan to harvest the tree.

Figure 7.—Completed overstory assessment tally sheet.

12

Culls and unacceptable growing-stock trees usually are removed first in a harvest. However, some may remain because they provide important habitat for wildlife or otherwise contribute to species diversity in the stand. For example, a butternut, even a cull one, is worth retaining.

Again, after determining the acceptability of a tallied tree, circle the coded symbol if the tree is marked for harvest, or, if the stand is unmarked, you plan to harvest the tree. Doing this will enable you to develop a picture of the residual forest stand following the harvest.

FIELD DATA SUMMARY

Once you have collected the data, you must summarize the information to understand the implications of the harvest relative to the stand. We will begin this process by first summarizing the regeneration data.

Summarizing Regeneration Data

Figure 8 is a sample regeneration tally sheet that you will develop as you work through this section.

Deer Impact

First, review the estimated deer impact for the stand. Use the deer impact to determine the regeneration threshold as shown in Table 3.

Advanced Regeneration

Using Table 3, determine which weighted number of seedlings is the appropriate threshold for this harvest area based on the deer impact. Determine the percentage of your plots that met or exceeded that threshold-weighted number of desirable seedlings.

Canopy Density

Add your plot-level estimates and record the total in the cell provided. Divide this number by the number of plots you evaluated to determine the average (see Figure 8).

Interference

Determine the percentage of the stand's plots that exceed the threshold for any interference. This is the percentage of the cells in Column 7 with a checkmark. For example, if you took five plots and four of them have checkmarks in Column 7, 80 percent of your plots have an interference problem.

If this percentage is at least 30 percent, you might want to summarize Columns 4, 5, and 6 in the same way to document which interfering plants are the source of the problem in the harvest area. Remember that even if grasses and sedges are present at levels below the threshold, their mere presence may indicate problems related to soil moisture and seed source.

In our example stand, Deer impact is estimated to be high (H, recorded in the "total" cell in the deer impact column). The regeneration threshold is 50 since it is a high deer-impact area. Two plots had a weighted seedling count of 50 or more (plots 3 and 4). Therefore, only 40 percent of the plots have adequate regeneration. In other words, advanced regeneration in this harvest area is inadequate.

The average canopy density is 40 percent. Therefore, this is a regeneration harvest, not a partial cut.

Fern cover is at least 30 percent on 80 percent of the understory plots. Grasses and sedges are less common than ferns and are less than the 30-percent threshold on any plot. Likewise, woody plants are not an issue; they are less than the 30-percent threshold on all five plots. Nonetheless, interference occurs on 80 percent of the plots.

13

Plot	1 Deer Impact (H/L)	2 Regen. Adequate	3 Canopy Density (percent)	4 Fern (percent)	5 Grasses/ sedges (percent)	6 Woody plants (percent)	7 Any Interference (check)
1		20	50	40	20	10	√
2		0	40	70	10	15	√
3		50+	40	40	0	5	√
4		50+	30	20	0	20	
5		10	40	30	20	10	√
		percent stocked	average percent	percent ≥ 30	percent ≥ 30	percent ≥ 30	percent with √
Stand	H	40	40	80	0	0	80

Figure 8.—Sample regeneration tally sheet showing all sample data.

Species Composition																	
Seed Source Total																	
Residual Quality																	

Species							Stand Summary			
Species Composition										
Seed Source Total							Priority Sp. Average		Stand Average	
Seed Source Average										
Residual Quality										
	# AGS Before After cut			# UGS Before After cut			Stand Diameter (+ or -)			
Overall Stand Quality										

Figure 9.—Overstory tally form summary data.

Summarizing Overstory Data

The rows at the bottom of the overstory tally form (Fig. 9) provide a place for summarizing the overstory data collected earlier. They will help you understand how decisions about harvesting affect the four critical variables mentioned previously: species composition, seed source, residual tree quality, and stand diameter.

Species Composition
Sustainable forestry implies retaining species composition. Diverse species composition ensures future management options and reflects consideration of wildlife, aesthetic, and other values. Some harvests reduce the number of tree species in a stand or remove too many trees of a particular species.

For example, across the Allegheny Plateau, black cherry is relatively easy to regenerate and may be the only valuable species that regenerates with high deer populations. Black cherry is a desirable species but we should exercise care that we do not develop stands dominated by single species (monocultures). Monocultures lack the resiliency of mixed-species stands because they may be at a higher risk for disease and insect injury.

In some cases it is desirable to reduce the abundance of individual tree species in a stand. There are occasions when species under threat of disease or insect outbreaks might be the focus of the harvest, for example, American beech when under attack by the beech bark

> **Species composition threshold:**
>
> If the harvest will eliminate a species or reduce its presence in the residual stand by more than 50 percent, species composition may be a concern.

scale complex. Some operations may include salvaging dead and dying trees. If there are concerns about a species that might create an interfering understory, e.g., black birch or black gum, you might also reduce it in a harvest.

If you maintain 50 percent or more of the individuals in that species in that size class, enter "0" in the species composition summary row of the tally sheet. Enter "–" if you reduced the number of individuals in the species by more than 50 percent in that size class. If there are no individuals of a species, leave the size classes blank for that species.

The lower portion of the tally sheet and the smaller summary table at the bottom aid in summarizing the information you have collected. Figure 10 displays the summary data for the example stand, demonstrating how the planned harvest will alter the stand. If a "–" is in half or more of the size classes in which that species occurred, record "–" for the stand.

Seed Source

Research has shown that 15 large to 30 small sawtimber-size black cherry trees per acre are necessary to successfully regenerate that species, and that a similar amount of red oak is adequate to ensure successful regeneration of that species. Similar data are not available for other species in Pennsylvania's forests. However, leaving 15 small to 30 large healthy sawtimber trees of each desired species per acre after harvest is a reasonably safe way to preserve the option of natural regeneration for those species. We want to ensure that the current harvest will leave sufficient seed source to regenerate desired species into the future. The only situation in which seed source does not matter is a regeneration harvest with well-established adequate regeneration and little or no interfering plants.

Identify the priority species, ideally through conversations with the landowner and forester, and ensure a seed source for that individual species. This should be the minimum residual stocking for stands in which regeneration is not already ensured. Retain additional healthy sawtimber trees for regeneration of other species. We will evaluate seed source using a weighted count of 30 per acre as the threshold. Large sawtimber trees, which generally produce more seed, are counted double. Since each of your plots is 1/10 acre, this threshold translates to an average of three trees per plot.

In the summary section at the bottom of the tally sheet, work with this variable only in the sawtimber size classes. For each species, record the weighted number of trees to be retained after harvest in the seed source total row. For small sawtimber trees, record the actual number of trees retained. For large sawtimber trees, record twice the number of trees retained as this class is weighted more heavily because these larger trees generally produce more seed.

In the row for seed source total in the stand summary block, record a weighted total equal to the number of small sawtimber trees plus the weighted number of large sawtimber trees. Divide these numbers by the number of plots taken and record this as the average seed source for each species in the row for seed source average.

In our example stand, there are reductions for BC in the small sawlog size class. Likewise, there were reductions for HE, RM, and BC in the large sawlog size class. For HE and RM, species that occur in only two size classes, there was a reduction in half of the size classes in which those species occurred, so each receives a "-" in the stand summary block.

BC occurred in three size classes and shows a reduction in two, so it, too, receives a "-" in the stand summary block. The 50-percent rule was violated for HE, RM, and BC.

BE occurs in three classes and had a reduction only in the largest one, so it receives a "0" in the stand summary block.

Owner: Jane Doe   Date: 6/10/03   Location: Logtown   Stand: 2

QUALITY (Q) — rows 30 down to 1

Instructions (right margin):

Enter species into the size class columns by order of tolerance, most tolerant to the left and most intolerant to the right.

Acceptable Growing Stock (AGS) code as "+" and Unacceptable Growing Stock (UGS) code as "-".

Remember to circle the code if the tree is marked or if the stand is unmarked and you plan to harvest the tree.

Species	HE	BE	SM	YB	RM	BC	HE	BE	SM	YB	RM	BC	HE	BE	SM	YB	RM	BC	HE	BE	SM	YB	RM	BC
Size Class	3 to 5.5 inches (saplings)						5.6 to 11.5 inches (poles)						11.6 to 17.5 inches (small saw)						17.6 inches or larger (large saw)					
Species Composition	0				0		0		0	0	0	-	-		0	0	0	-						-
Seed Source Total				1									3		3	1	4							
Residual Quality	0				0		0		0	0	0	0	0		0	0	0	+						0

Species	HE	BE	SM	YB	RM	BC
Species Composition	-	0	0	0	0	-
Seed Source Total			3	1	4	3
Seed Source Average	.6		.2	.2	.8	.6
Residual Quality	0	0	+		0	0

	#AGS		#UGS	
	Before cut	After cut	Before cut	After cut
Overall Stand Quality	64	23	51	46

Stand Summary

	Priority Sp. Average	Stand Average
	species reduced	
	1.2	2.2
	sugar maple improved	
Stand Diameter (+ or –)	proportion of UGS increased	

Figure 10.—Overstory assessment tally sheet with stand summary data.

In the sample stand, the overstory tally is based on five plots, so we divide by five. Finally, in the stand summary cell, record the average for the priority species and for the stand. In the sample stand, black cherry and sugar maple are the priority species. The planned harvest leaves three black cherry, four red maple, one yellow birch, and three sugar maple, all in the small sawtimber class. Thus, our total residual is 6 priority trees and 11 total residual sawtimber trees, or an average of about 1 priority tree per plot (6/5 = 1.2) and about 2 (11/5 = 2.2) sawtimber trees per plot. Both of these totals are below the threshold for seed source.

Residual Tree Quality

In a timber harvest, it is easy to focus only on the trees to be removed. Sustainable forestry also focuses on residual trees—those retained after the harvest. Following a harvest, the residual stand should contain a higher proportion of quality trees of desirable species relative to the original stand conditions. But the residual stand also should include two to five trees with obvious internal or external defects or other health problems. These trees are left to preserve species composition (as a seed source), and/or as cavities or snags (standing dead trees) for wildlife. However, it is possible to leave too many trees of undesirable quality. Such trees may occupy too much of the next forest and interfere with the growth of desirable residual trees or regeneration.

What will the harvest do to residual tree quality? Record your interpretations by species and size class in the residual tree quality row of the tally sheet (Fig. 10, Row 3). Enter "0" if you did not change the relative proportion of AGS to UGS, "−" if you increased the proportion of UGS to AGS, or "+" if you improved the proportion of AGS to UGS.

Then, for each species assess the change across all size classes in the stand (Fig.10, Row 7). Enter "0" if you did not change the relative proportion of AGS to UGS, "−" if the proposed cut increased the proportion of UGS to AGS, or "+" if you improved the proportion of AGS to UGS.

Continuing with the example in Figure 10 (refer to the SM column in the small sawlog size class), we see that the relative proportion of AGS to UGS has improved. Record "+" in the small sawtimber sugar maple cell in the summary block at the bottom of the tally sheet. For sugar maple, there was no change in relative quality in the sapling and pole classes, so record "0" in each of those cells and leave the large sawtimber sugar maple cell blank since there are no sugar maple trees in that size class. In the stand summary block, record "+" for sugar maple since the overall impact of the harvest will be to increase the proportion of sugar maple AGS in the stand. Leave cells blank if a species was removed in that size class, e.g., beech in small sawtimber and red maple in large sawtimber. In the sample stand, black cherry receives a blank in saplings (there were none) and in large sawtimber (the species was eliminated). In poles and small sawtimber, black cherry receives a "0" because all of the black cherry were AGS before the harvest, and only black cherry AGS remain after the harvest in these categories. For the stand as a whole, then, black cherry receives a "0."

> **Relative residual tree quality threshold:**
>
> The intent is to increase the relative proportion of good quality trees (i.e., AGS to UGS) after the timber harvest.

On the bottom line, record the number of AGS and UGS in the stand as a whole both before and after harvest. Consider any changes in the proportion of AGS to UGS in the stand. By species, apparently there was little change in residual tree quality for the stand. Sugar maple actually improved while the other species showed no change. However, the overall occurrence of UGS increased relative to AGS. Before our sample harvest there were 64 AGS and 51 UGS (more AGS than UGS, both nearly half the stand). After harvest, there were twice as many UGS as AGS, and all of the AGS were removed from the larger diameter class.

Average Stand Diameter

The stand's average d.b.h. helps us understand and interpret shifts in the distribution of tree size following harvesting. How will the harvest affect stand structure? Will the harvest take trees from both large- and small-diameter classes? How will this cut affect the next harvest and the stand's regeneration? It is important for growth potential, financial value, wildlife habitat, and aesthetic character of forests.

Will the harvest take trees from both large and small diameter classes? In many Pennsylvania stands, there is a wide range of tree diameters and heights. Sometimes this is due to difference ages within the stand, but more often, it is due to differences is species growth rates and the stand is actually even-aged. Within the stand, the fastest growing species tend to have diameters that are greater than those of trees of the same age from slower growing species. Within a species, the fastest growing individuals have the largest diameters.

For example, in cherry-maple forests of the Allegheny Plateau, it is common to find an 18-inch, 90-year-old black cherry growing next to a 12-inch, 90-year-old sugar maple. If we harvest primarily the smaller trees in the stand, we increase the average stand diameter and leave the fastest growing individuals to continue growth. If we harvest primarily the larger trees, we reduce average stand diameter and leave slower growing individuals. We also change the distribution of foliage in the stand and the amount and quality of light reaching the regeneration on the forest floor as well as the character of wildlife habitat in the stand.

In even-aged forests, an improvement harvest (crown partial cut) in which competing trees are removed to create growing space for residual trees should maintain or increase the average stand diameter. In uneven-aged forests, selection harvest should cut throughout the diameter distribution, leaving the average diameter essentially unchanged. The harvest operation should emphasize leaving high-quality, vigorous trees. Whether the harvest is a selection or a partial cut, the goal is to improve the stand for future harvests.

How will this cut affect the next harvest? Harvests that increase stand diameter or leave it unchanged result in a residual stand that is growing as fast or faster than before the harvest. If the increase in stand diameter was accompanied by creation of conditions

Stand structure is the distribution of tree sizes across the harvest area— tree diameter, height, and foliage distribution.

Average stand diameter threshold:

Concerns should be raised if the average stand diameter decreases by more than 10 percent, e.g., the average stand diameter before the cut is 16 inches and 14 inches after the cut.

good for regeneration, a final harvest of desirable composition and value is likely in the near future.

In uneven-aged stands with diameters unchanged by harvest, volume growth should continue steadily as before the harvest. However, diameter-limit harvests that remove primarily large trees leave a forest that looks younger than it is because the heights and diameters of the residual trees are smaller than before the harvest. The growth rates of trees that are left behind will be slower than those of trees that were cut. The severity of this decrease in growth rate depends on the severity of the cut, and on residual species composition and quality. In cases of high-grading, the practice of removing the largest and most valuable trees, stand growth can be set back and recovery of harvestable products from the tract in the future delayed for many decades.

How will this harvest affect the stand's regeneration potential? Cuts not intended as regeneration harvests—those with residual canopy closure of at least 50 percent—still have important consequences for regeneration potential in the harvested stand. If average diameter is increased through the cutting, more light will reach the forest floor to stimulate the germination and growth of advanced seedlings. If the average diameter is reduced because only the largest trees are harvested, low-shade conditions may be created that delay or prevent regeneration establishment and growth.

High-grading is removing only the largest and most valuable trees in a stand.

Appendix A includes a detailed procedure for estimating change in average stand diameter. We suggest a graphical method for determining the impact of the planned harvest on average diameter. Use a pencil and the overstory assessment tally sheet (Fig. 11) to make this determination. Mentally total up the tolerant and midtolerant species in each size class, including both the trees you plan to leave and cut (the "+" and "-" with or without circles), and draw a solid free-form curve that represents the distribution of these species through the size classes.

For example, in the sample stand the free-form curve would start with 25 saplings, go off the chart completely in the poletimber class, with 18 sugar maple, 1 hemlock, and 13 beech, and fall to 11 and 8 in the small and large sawtimber, respectively. Draw a similar curve for the intolerant species, starting from the other end. In the sample stand, this curve would start with 15 black cherry in the large sawtimber class, 23 black cherry in the small sawtimber class, and 1 black cherry in the pole class. Visually estimate the average diameter based on these two curves—for the sample stand, somewhere near the low end of the small sawtimber class, around 11 inches.

Now make two more curves (Fig. 12), counting only those trees scheduled as residuals after the planned harvest (the symbols that are not circled). Lightly shade in the differences between the two curves to indicate the harvest planned, and again visually estimate the average diameter in the sample stand. In the example, where the entire harvest is scheduled to occur is in the sawtimber classes, it would fall to the lower end of the poletimber class, around 8 inches. This is much more than a 10-percent drop in

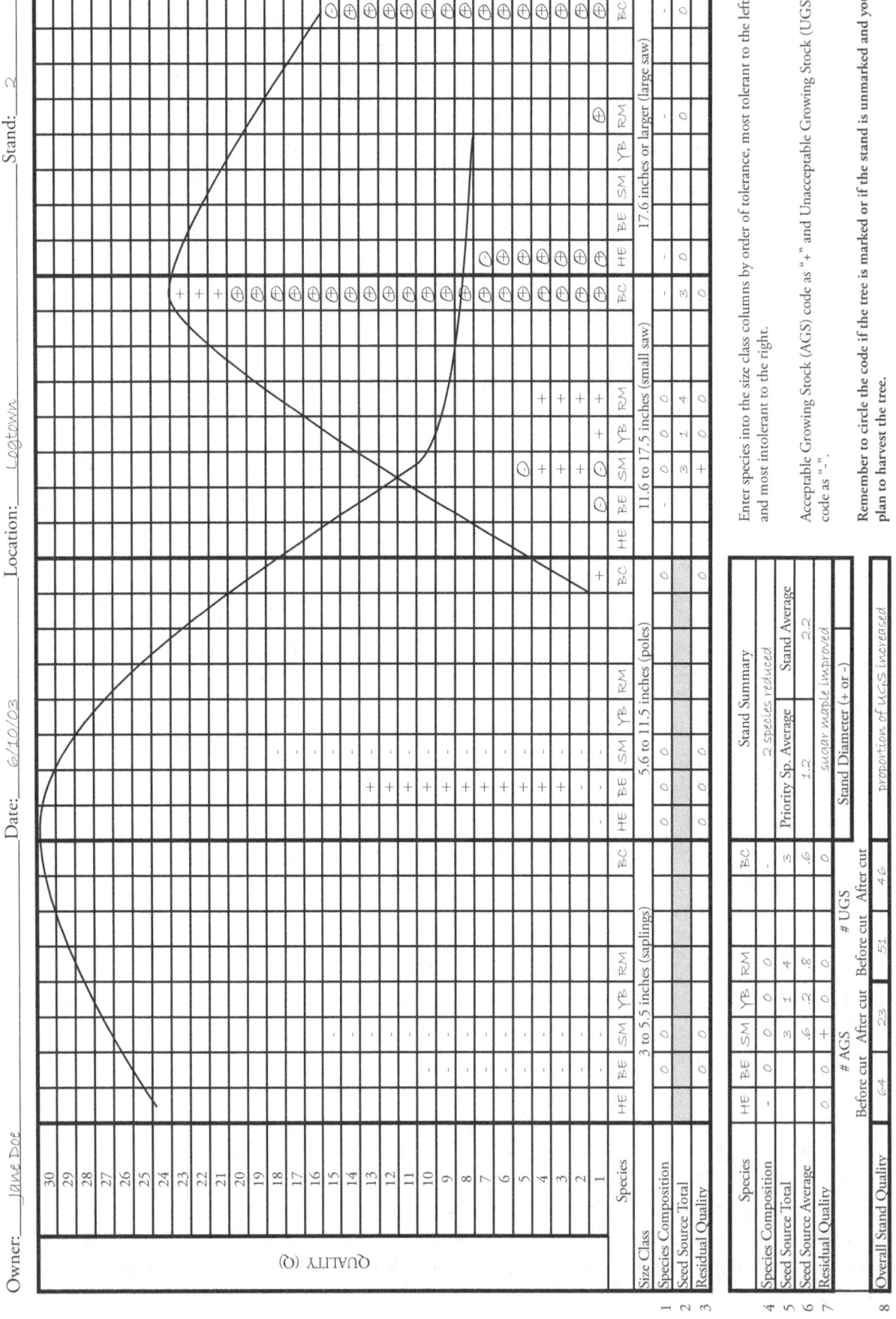

Figure 11.—Overstory assessment tally sheet with preharvest curve and stand summary data.

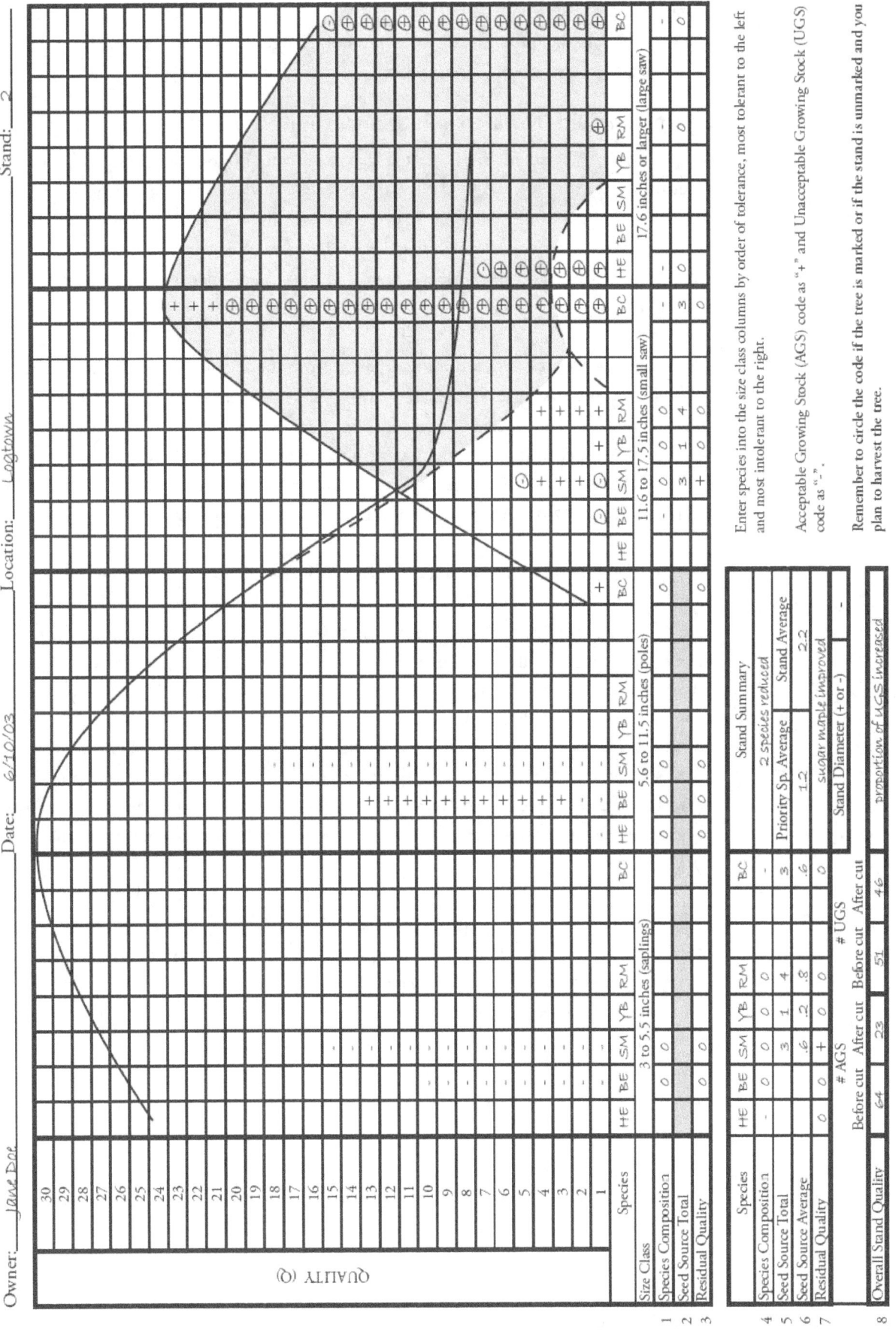

Figure 12.—Oversory assessment tally sheet with residual tree d.b.h. curves and trees scheduled for removal shaded.

average diameter, so record "–" in the stand diameter row of the summary block (note in Appendix A that the more precise calculation of change in average diameter from these data suggest a reduction of 27 percent).

Interpreting the Overstory Assessment Tally Sheet

The Overstory Assessment Tally Sheet (Fig. 12) provides important information for determining whether the planned harvest will yield a sustainable outcome. Specifically, we are interested in understanding what the harvest will do to species composition, seed source, residual tree quality, and average stand diameter. We want to retain or improve species composition and tree quality, retain seed source, and increase or maintain average stand diameter.

The stand in Figure 12 is significantly different from the one we inventoried. It is clear that the harvest is taking all of the large sawlog trees and nearly all of the small sawlog trees. Some of the SM and RM are retained in the residuals but nearly all of the BC, an important tree species in this stand, has been removed resulting in a stand of low quality BE and SM. All of the HE in the large sawlog size class have been removed. Quality of the residual stand is evident from the number of "-" symbols relative to "+" symbols.

We have changed this stand by reducing species diversity (reducing the amount of BC and HE), and the overall quality (the residual forests has many more low quality trees because we took all those AGS in the larger size classes). Also, the average stand diameter has dropped considerably, an estimated 3 inches or 27 percent (see Appendix A).

The Sustainability Key

Using the sustainability key in Figure 13 along with the regeneration data from Figure 8 and summarized overstory data in Figure 12, we can determine whether the proposed harvest will achieve a sustainable outcome. As shown, the sustainability key asks a series of paired questions or couplets that relate to the harvesting decisions you made for the stand.

The first item relates to the estimated residual overstory density. If it is less than 50 percent, which it is, the planned harvest is a regeneration cut and we move to item 2. Less than 70 percent of the plots have adequate advanced regeneration so we move to item 6. Looking at the summary stand data in Figure 12, we see that the seed source is inadequate; two species were lost or reduced (HE and BC), and our stand average is 2.2 trees/acre in small and large sawtimber to provide seed source in a stand that already lacks adequate advanced regeneration. The key tells us to delay the harvest and seek assistance.

	Item	Description	Go To:
	1	Residual overstory canopy > 50% (partial cut)	Go to
		Residual overstory canopy ≤ 50% (regeneration cut)	Go to 2
	2	Advance regeneration < 70%	Go to 6
		Advance regeneration ≥ 70%	Go to 3
Regeneration harvest Advanced regeneration present, abundant	3	Percent plots stocked with interfering vegetation overtopping desirable regeneration ≥ 70%	Go to 4
		Percent plots stocked with interfering vegetation overtopping desirable regeneration < 70%	Go to 5
	4	Interference treatment planned in conjunction with harvest	Go to 5
		Interference treatment not planned	Delay harvest. Seek assistance
	5	Deer impact low or deer impact reduction planned (fencing or very aggressive hunting)	Treat and harvest. Follow up stand development. Probably sustainable.
		Deer impact high and no deer impact treatment planned	Seek assistance. Will seedlings overwhelm deer?
Regeneration harvest Advanced regeneration scarce or absent	6	One or more desirable seed source species lost or reduced in overstory to < 15 large or 30 small sawlog trees per acre with strong crowns	Delay harvest. Seek assistance.
		Desirable seed source species ≥ 15 large or 30 small sawlog trees with strong crowns retained	Go to 7
	7	Fern ≥ 30% of 30% plots	Go to 10
		Fern < 30% on 30% of plots	Go to 8
	8	Grass/sedge ≥ 30% on 30% of plots	Go to 10
		Grass/sedge < 30% on 30% of plots	Go to 9
	9	Woody interference ≥ 30% of 30% plots	Go to 10
		Woody interference < 30% on 30% of plots	Go to 10

Figure 13.—Sustainability key.

	Item	Description	Go To:
	10	All interfering plants ≥ 30% on 30% of plots	Go to 11
		All interfering plants < 30% on 30% of plots	Go to 12
	11	Interference treatment planned with harvest	Go to 12
		Interference treatment not planned	Delay harvest. Desirable seedlings not likely to be competitive after harvest. Seek assistance.
	12	Deer impact low or deer impact reduction planned (fencing or aggressive hunting)	Treat and harvest. Follow up stand development. Probably sustainable.
		Deer impact high and no deer impact treatment planned	Delay harvest. Scarce seedlings likely to disappear after harvest. Seek assistance.
Partial cut Check seed source	13	One or more desirable seed source species lost or reduced in overstory to < 15 large or 30 small sawlog trees per acre with strong crowns	Delay harvest. Seek assistance.
		Desirable seed source species ≥ 15 large or 30 small sawlog trees with strong crowns retained	Go to 14
Partial cut Seed source adequate Check residual stand	14	Average DBH retained or increased (≤ 10% reduction)	Rate of growth likely sustained or improved. Go to 15.
		Average DBH reduced (> 10% reduction)	Rate of growth likely slowed. Go to 15
	15	Timber quality sustained or improved by harvest, average DBH retained or increased	Future valuable harvest probable. Probably sustainable.
		Timber quality sustained or improved by harvest, average DBH reduced	Future valuable harvest probable, though later than with diameter improvement. Probably sustainable.
		Timber quality reduced by best trees removed and/or damage to residual, ≥ 15 large or 30 small sawlog trees with strong crowns retained as seed source	Future valuable harvest at risk. May not be sustainable. Consider regenerating

Figure 13.—continued.

Alternative Treatment

Figure 14 suggests an alternative treatment for this stand. The proposed harvest still will take some of the small and large BC sawlogs, but not all. This way, we retain the seed source and we have a potential for cherry in the future stand if we control for the interfering plants identified in the regeneration assessment. We have retained some of the larger HE and RM, improved the SM by cutting UGS, and put more of the operation into the smaller diameter classes, improving overall stand quality, retaining species composition, and maintaining or increasing stand diameter.

Owner: _Jane Doe_   Date: _6/10/03_   Location: _Logtown_   Stand: _2_

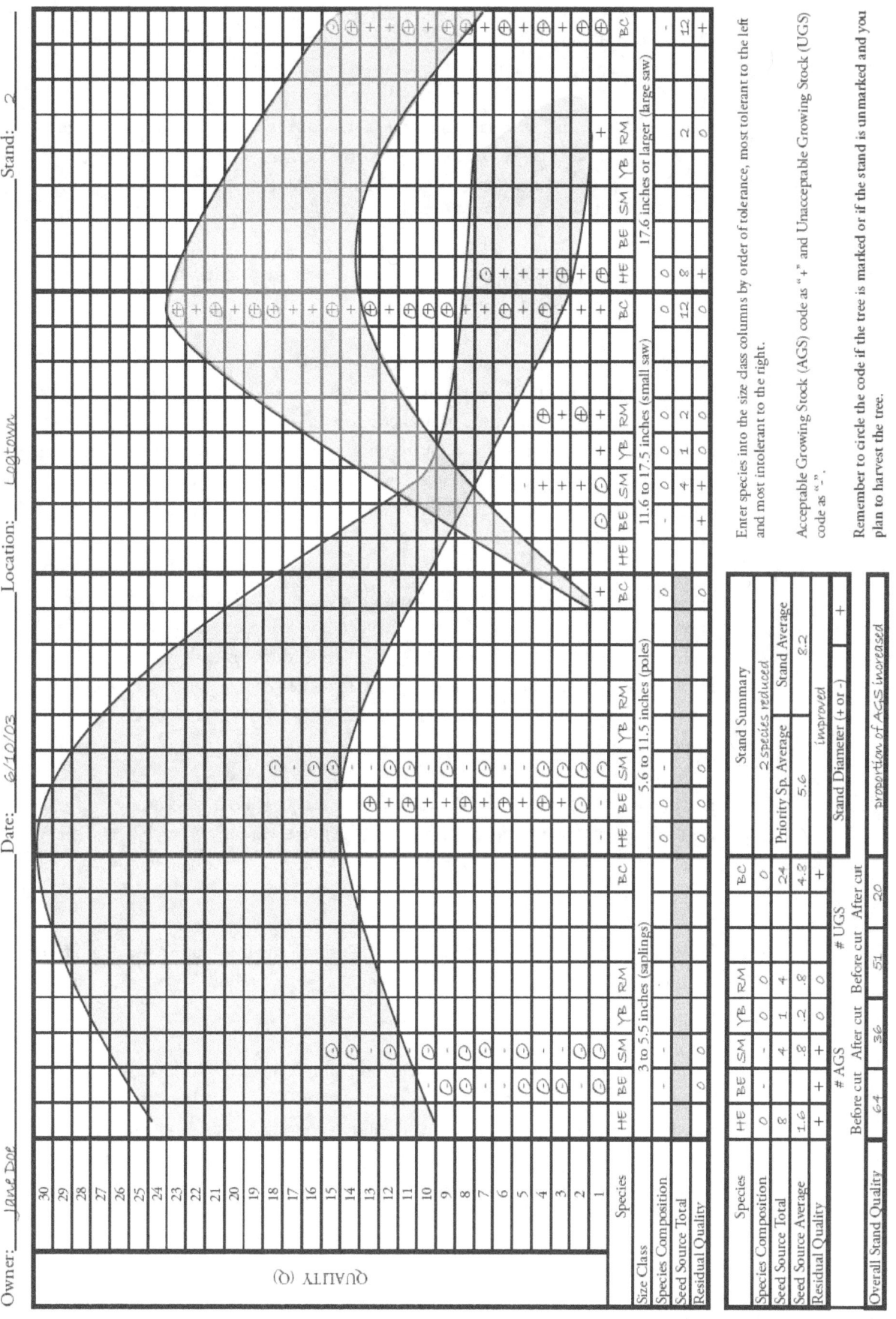

Enter species into the size class columns by order of tolerance, most tolerant to the left and most intolerant to the right.

Acceptable Growing Stock (AGS) code as " + " and Unacceptable Growing Stock (UGS) code as " - ".

Remember to circle the code if the tree is marked or if the stand is unmarked and you plan to harvest the tree.

Figure 14.— Alternative cut.

25

This harvest does not produce as much immediate income but the next harvest will have additional value, and we have protected our options for regenerating the stand. Now work it through the sustainability key, starting with item 6.

Since we are retaining adequate seed source, we would move to item 7. From Figure 8, we know that fern cover exceeds the 30-percent threshold on 80 percent of the plots, so we would be instructed to go to item 10 where the question relates to any interference. The summary data in Figure 8 column 7, any interference, again indicate that interference occurs on 80 percent of the plots. The key sends us to item 11, where we encounter a major concern—we have an interference problem that will result in an unsustainable harvest outcome.

If no treatment to control interfering plants is planned, we should seek assistance. If a treatment to control interfering plants is planned, we are instructed to go to item 12, where we need to consider deer—another barrier to successful regeneration. If the deer impact is low or fencing or aggressive hunting are planned, we can treat the stand for interfering vegetation and deer impact and harvest. With follow up, the stand probably is sustainable, but if deer impact is high or no control is planned, we are instructed to delay the harvest and seek assistance.

When treating interfering plants, it is important to understand that the herbicide or mechanical treatment may destroy existing advanced regeneration, and that the treatment must be given time to be effective. After treating interfering plants and waiting for the treatment to take effect, it is essential to collect new understory data and to start with item 2. It is essential for a sustainable harvest to have regeneration conditions that ensure that the next forest is in place.

Finally, obtaining a sustainable outcome from a timber harvest depends on protecting the residual stand and having adequate advanced regeneration. When harvesting a stand, especially during a partial or improvement cut, you are attempting to ensure that future generations have high-quality trees to harvest.

Do everything you can to make sure that you protect the trees you are leaving. Practice directional felling; avoid hitting the stems and crowns of residual trees to the extent possible.

Use bumper trees along skid trails, skid roads, and haul roads to protect the trunks of trees you intend to keep. Depending on the harvest, consider bucking stems in the woods into shorter lengths. When feasible, limit barking by harvesting during the dormant season, rather than when trees are actively growing. Information on BMPs is available from your cooperative extension office, Bureau of Forestry, or Pennsylvania SFI office.

It is easy to focus on the condition of the residual stems but also be aware of what is occurring below ground to the roots of these trees. Skidding damage occurs to roots primarily through soil compaction. Harvesting when soils are wet can significantly increase root damage to residual trees. Skidding without a plan increases the overall disturbance in the stand and can lead to excessive root damage and soil disturbance. Plan the harvest operation before starting.

WHAT HAVE WE LEARNED?

Coming away from this program, you now can differentiate between a partial cut and regeneration cut. With respect to regeneration cuts, you can evaluate sites that will pose problems and those that will produce sustainable forests. You now are aware of barriers that interfere with regeneration and know when to seek assistance when problems arise.

Remember to seek assistance when there is a species loss, a major drop in average stand d.b.h., or when you suspect regeneration problems (such as an overabundance of ferns or too many undesirable woody plants).

You also can evaluate the quality of the residual trees. With simple data-collection tools, you can describe species composition, estimate diameter distribution by species, evaluate crown closure, and understand the effect of light on tree growth and regeneration.

It is the hope of all of us working with Pennsylvania's forests that by using these skills you will earn a more professional image and improve relationships with the public, forest-land owners, foresters, and other loggers. Our mutual goal is to sustain our valuable timber resources and forest products industry. To obtain this goal, we need to work together.

ADDITIONAL RESOURCES

Appendices B and C provide additional information that you might find helpful. Appendix B includes blank overstory and understory inventory sheets. Appendix C includes SFI's timber harvesting assessment and treatment unit sustainability assessment forms. Both forms are designed to summarize postharvest conditions on a property. Information on BMPs for Pennsylvania forests is featured in the Forest Stewardship Bulletin that is reprinted at the end of this report.

APPENDIX A
ESTIMATING AVERAGE STAND DIAMETER

Figures 15 and 16 provide a way to rapidly estimate average stand diameter from the data entered in Figure 7. Since we have not recorded the actual diameters for each tree (we are working with diameter classes), we only can estimate the change in average diameter. It is obvious from Figure 10 that the cut focused on large trees, so we expect the those trees left in the stand will be smaller on average. We can roughly estimate the change in average diameter by using the average diameter for each of the size classes we used to record the trees tallied (i.e., saplings, poles, and small sawlogs, and the small end of the large sawlog class). Because the calculation of average stand diameter is based on averages for size classes, it is not as sensitive as it would be in a normal cruise. Nonetheless, it can provide a rough estimate of the amount and direction of the diameter shift.

Size Class	Pre-Harvest Tree Total by size classes	Multiplier	(Sum this column)
Sapling (3-5.5 in)		X 4.0	=
Poles (5.6-11.5 in)		X 8.5	=
Small sawlogs (11.6-17.5 in)		X 14.5	=
Large sawlogs (>17.5 in)		X 17.5	=
Total	(B)		= (A)
		Average DBH = A ÷ B	
	$\dfrac{(A)}{(B)}$ =	Pre-Harvest Average DBH	(PRE)

Size Class	Post-Harvest Tree Total by size classes	Multiplier	(Sum this column)
Sapling (3-5.5 in)		X 4.0	=
Poles (5.6-11.5 in)		X 8.5	=
Small sawlogs (11.6-17.5 in)		X 14.5	=
Large sawlogs (>17.5 in)		X 17.5	=
Total	(B)		= (A)
		Average DBH = A ÷ B	
	$\dfrac{(A)}{(B)}$ =	Post-Harvest Average DBH	(POST)

$$\frac{Post\text{-}Harvest\ Diameter - Pre\text{-}Harvest\ Diameter}{Pre\text{-}Harvest\ Diameter} \times 100 = Percent\ Change\ in\ Diameter$$

$$\frac{POST\ (\quad\quad) - PRE\ (\quad\quad)}{PRE\ (\quad\quad)} \times 100 = Percent\ Change\ in\ Diameter$$

Figure 15.—Diameter distribution summary worksheet.

Figure 15 is a worksheet for computing the direction and for estimating the percentage change in average diameter in a marked stand using data in Figure 7. Figure 16 shows the completed example using data from Figure 8. It often is possible to estimate the preharvest and postharvest diameter distributions by examining the overstory data sheet. However, it takes little time to complete the diameter distribution summary sheet and this exercise is useful for understanding how cutting changes stand characteristics. In Figure 16, we see that the preharvest average diameter is 11.1 inches. If we follow the marking instructions indicated by the plusses and minuses in Figure 7, the postharvest average diameter drops to 8.1 inches, a 27-percent decrease in average stand diameter. This large drop is clearly attributed to the removal of all of the trees in the large sawlog class and nearly all in the small sawlog group. Note that there was no intentional thinning in the smaller diameter classes.

Size Class	Pre-Harvest Tree Total by size classes	Multiplier	(Sum this column)
Sapling (3-5.5 in)	25	X 4.0	= 100
Poles (5.6-11.5 in)	33	X 8.5	= 280.5
Small sawlogs (11.6-17.5 in)	34	X 14.5	= 493
Large sawlogs (>17.5 in)	23	X 17.5	= 402.5
Total	115 **(B)**		= 1276 **(A)**
		Average DBH = A ÷ B	

$$\frac{(A)\ \ 115}{(B)\ \ 1276} = 11.1 \quad \text{Pre-Harvest Average DBH} \quad \text{(PRE)}$$

Size Class	Post-Harvest Tree Total by size classes	Multiplier	(Sum this column)
Sapling (3-5.5 in)	25	X 4.0	= 100
Poles (5.6-11.5 in)	33	X 8.5	= 280.5
Small sawlogs (11.6-17.5 in)	10	X 14.5	= 145
Large sawlogs (>17.5 in)	0	X 17.5	= 0
Total	65 **(B)**		= 525.5 **(A)**
		Average DBH = A ÷ B	

$$\frac{(A)\ \ 65}{(B)\ \ 525.5} = 8.1 \quad \text{Post-Harvest Average DBH} \quad \text{(POST)}$$

$$\frac{\text{Post-Harvest Diameter} - \text{Pre-Harvest Diameter}}{\text{Pre-Harvest Diameter}} \times 100 = \text{Percent Change in Diameter}$$

$$\frac{\text{POST}\ (8.1) - \text{PRE}\ (11.1)}{\text{PRE}\ (11.1)} \times 100 = -27$$

Figure 16. —Sample diameter distribution summary.

APPENDIX B
UNDERSTORY AND OVERSTORY TALLY SHEETS

Plot	1 Deer Impact (H/L)	7 Regen. Adequate	2 Canopy Density (%)	3 Fern (%)	4 Grasses/ Sedges (%)	5 Woody Plants (%)	6 Any Inter- ference (Check)
1							
2							
3							
4							
5							
6							
7							
8							
9							
10							
11							
12							
13							
14							
15							
16							
17							
18							
19							
20							
		percent stocked	average percent	percent ≥ 30	percent ≥ 30	percent ≥ 30	percent with √
Stand							

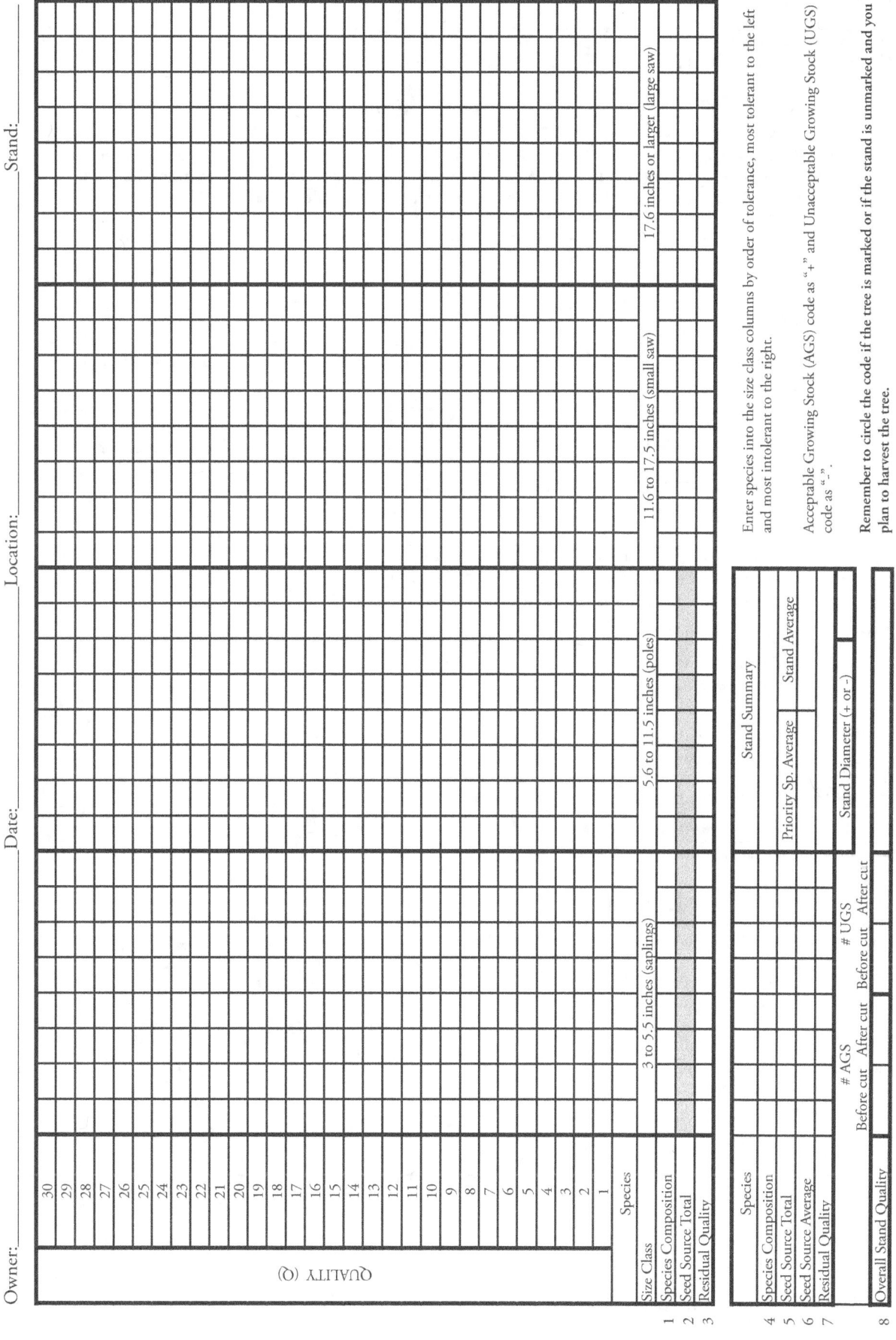

Owner: _____ Date: _____ Location: _____ Stand: _____

QUALITY (Q)

Row labels: 30, 29, 28, 27, 26, 25, 24, 23, 22, 21, 20, 19, 18, 17, 16, 15, 14, 13, 12, 11, 10, 9, 8, 7, 6, 5, 4, 3, 2, 1

Species

Size Class	3 to 5.5 inches (saplings)	5.6 to 11.5 inches (poles)	11.6 to 17.5 inches (small saw)	17.6 inches or larger (large saw)
1 Species Composition				
2 Seed Source Total				
3 Residual Quality				

Species

4 Species Composition		
5 Seed Source Total		
6 Seed Source Average		
7 Residual Quality		

	# AGS		# UGS	
	Before cut	After cut	Before cut	After cut
8 Overall Stand Quality				

Stand Summary

Priority Sp. Average	Stand Average

Stand Diameter (+ or –)

Enter species into the size class columns by order of tolerance, most tolerant to the left and most intolerant to the right.

Acceptable Growing Stock (AGS) code as "+" and Unacceptable Growing Stock (UGS) code as "–".

Remember to circle the code if the tree is marked or if the stand is unmarked and you plan to harvest the tree.

APPENDIX C
TIMBER HARVESTING ASSESSMENT AND TREATMENT
UNIT SUSTAINABILITY ASSESSMENT FORMS

SUSTAINABLE FORESTRY INITIATIVE® OF PENNSYLVANIA
TREATMENT UNIT SUSTAINABILITY ASSESSMENT FORM

Harvests may include multiple treatment units. For example, the harvest might include a 10-acre unit to release regeneration and a 40-acre stand improvement unit. A separate Treatment Unit Sustainability Assessment Forms (TUSAF) should be completed for each treatment unit. Attach all TUSAF forms to the single Timber Harvesting Assessment form for the area. *(All detailed landowner, location and contractor information provided on the (TUSAF) form will be kept confidential by the SFI of PA office. Forms tallied for analytical purposes will be identified numerically and will not contain specific names or locations.)*

This form is for Unit # _____ **of** _____

Township of Harvest _____

County of Harvest _____

Total Harvest Acres _____

Treatment Unit Acres _____

% of Unit Harvested _____

Dates of Harvest _____

Assessment Date _____

Product Destination _____

Harvesting Company _____

TUSAF Assessor(s) _____

Landowner _____

Person to contact for follow-up information or to schedule a site visit:

Name: _____

Address: _____

City, State, Zip: _____

Phone: _____

E-mail: _____

Signature: _____ **Date** _____

---

1. Who developed the harvest recommendation and prescription?
__ Landowner or Landowners family   __ Landowner's Forester   __ Buyer's Forester
__ Timber Harvester / Logger   __ Timber Buyer   __ Other _____

---

2. What ownership category best describes the current owner?
__ Private forest landowner owning _____ acres in PA.
__ Industrial forest landowner
__ Forest investment owner
__ Municipal
__ State
__ Federal

---

3. Is this harvest associated with conversion to non-forest use?
__ Yes   __ No   If yes, what?_____

Please refer to the diagram below when answering questions 4 and 5 for trees 6 inches DBH and larger.

---

4. Estimate the percent <u>summer</u> canopy closure that best describes the unit prior to harvest?

__ Greater than 75%   __ 51 to 75%
__ 26 to 50%   __ Less than 25%

Estimate % Canopy Cover for Trees Six (6) Inches DBH and Larger (only)

40%   80%
20%   60%

5. Estimate the percent <u>summer</u> canopy closure that best describes the unit after harvest?

__ Greater than 75%   __ 51 to 75%
__ 26 to 50%   __ Less than 25%

Return to: Sustainable Forestry Initiative of Pennsylvania
315 South Allen Street, #418, State College, PA 16801

6. How did the harvest affect the average tree diameter? __ The average diameter increased (many to most of the trees cut were smaller than the average tree size before harvest) __ The average diameter remained the same __ The average diameter decreased (many to most of the trees cut were larger than the average tree size before harvest) __ N/A overstory removed
7. Did the harvest result in a change of timber quality in the residual stand? __ Timber quality improved (most of the trees cut were of below-average quality) __ Timber quality remained the same __ Timber quality decreased (a majority of the high-quality stems were removed or damaged during the harvest and lesser quality stems predominate in the remaining stand) __ N/A (overstory removal)
8. How has the harvest affected the species composition of the overstory? __ The percent of medium to low value species decreased __The percent of medium to high value species decreased __ The percent species composition remained relatively unchanged. N/A (overstory removal)
Answer questions 9 – 14 if the residual overstory canopy closure after harvest will be less than 50% (see question 5).
9. Estimate the percent of the area stocked with advanced desirable seedlings (rooted in mineral soil) and vigorous saplings. __Less than 10%   _ 10 to 30%   __ 31 to 50%   __ 51 to 70%   __ Greater than 70%
10. Estimate the percent of the area covered with interfering plants including ferns, grasses/sedges, and/or woody non-commercial species (such as beech, black locust, fire cherry, striped maple, rhododenron, mountain laurel). Less than 10%   10 to 30%   31 to 50%   51 to 70%   Greater than 70%
11. Are the seedlings/saplings in question 9 overtopped by the interfering vegetation? __ On less than 10% of the area   __ On 10 to 30%   __ On 31 to 50% __ 51 to 70%   __ On greater than 70%
12. Is an interfering plant treatment that conserves seedlings planned in association with this harvest? Yes – Describe treatment and schedule _____   No
13. What is the expected deer impact on regeneration in this treatment unit? _____ __ High   __Medium   __Low
14. Is there a plan to mitigate deer impact?   __ Yes   __ No   If yes, mark all that apply: __ Fence   __ Fertilization   __ DMAP (Additional Hunting)   __ Other _____

Return to: Sustainable Forestry Initiative of Pennsylvania
315 South Allen Street, #418, State College, PA 16801

Text reprinted with permission from Penn State College of Agricultural Sciences.
Artwork reprinted with permission from Patrick Britten.

Forest Stewardship
Best Management Practices for Pennsylvania Forests

Best Management Practices (BMPs) for silvicultural activities in forested wetlands and for controlling erosion and sedimentation from timber harvesting operations have been established for Pennsylvania forests. (See references, pages 7 and 9.) The BMPs outlined in this bulletin supplement existing BMPs to benefit a wider array of forest resources and values. They reflect what we know today about ensuring forest sustainability.

A 48-page booklet, *Best Management Practices for Pennsylvania Forests*, includes additional information about Pennsylvania forests, ecological principles and processes, the role of timber harvesting, silvicultural practices, forest protection and health, and rules and regulations affecting timber harvesting activities. The booklet is available through the Pennsylvania Department of Conservation and Natural Resources (DCNR) Bureau of Forestry and Penn State Cooperative Extension.

This publication is written under the assumption that voluntary compliance with BMPs, reinforced with education, will serve all of us better in the long run, both economically and socially. In practical terms, voluntary compliance in implementing BMPs can help avoid the establishment of additional regulatory statutes, many of which can be burdensome, time consuming, costly, and not necessarily conducive to long-term forest health and productivity.

BMPs are universally accepted activities that have positive effects or minimize negative effects on the forest ecosystem. Their impacts can be limited to individual stands or spread over multiple ownerships.

Some BMPs are multipurpose. For example, *buffer strips* along streams designed to control sedimentation can also serve as wildlife travel corridors, result in habitat diversity, and maintain stream water temperature and nutrient levels.

BMPs must remain flexible over time, to accommodate changes in the social, economic, and environmental contexts of forest resource use. Our education in this area must be ongoing.

The BMPs provide the basics—minimal acceptable standards—of good forest management, although some landowners may choose to do more. You will probably want to review the information in this publication with the natural resource professionals who help you manage your land.

The Best Management Practices that follow are divided into three areas of forest management: planning, forest operations, and forest values. Each forest resource management component includes an objective, the primary issue upon which the BMPs are based, considerations and concerns regarding the management component, and a checklist of BMPs that address those considerations and concerns. The checklist is provided in general terms. You can get detailed information from the publications listed at the end of each management component, under "For Additional Information."

HIGH-GRADING

There is concern among all sectors of the forestry community that high-grading—the harvesting of only those trees that will give the highest immediate economic return—may lead to a widespread decline in forest resource quality. Two practices, diameter-limit cutting and selective cutting, generally fall into this category. In diameter-limit cutting, all saleable trees above a certain diameter are harvested. Selective cutting usually removes the largest, most valuable trees and may leave large-diameter, poor-quality, low-value trees. In each case, most of the trees that remain after the harvest are genetically inferior or physically defective. Neither method gives any thought to the composition of the future forest.

In even-aged forests such as those in Pennsylvania, smaller-diameter trees are not necessarily younger trees. It is more probable that these smaller trees are:

1. slow-growing species of the same age as different, fast-growing species;

2. the same species of the same age but growing on an inferior microsite; or

3. the same species of the same age but genetically inferior to their larger -diameter counterparts.

Because slower-growing and poor-quality trees are retained, high-grading diminishes the diversity and economic value of the future forest. Landowners may agree to high-grading because of a lack of knowledge about the practice and its undesirable consequences. High-grading also can be driven by short-term economic considerations. Immediate cash flow may be higher with high-grading, but potential environmental degradation and decreased future timber values will more than cancel the immediate cash advantage.

Stewardship requires that landowners consider the future consequences of high-grading when making a decision whether or not to accept the use of the practice on their land. Resource professionals and harvesters also have an obligation to look beyond the present when recommending forest management practices to landowners.

Definitions for italicized terms not explained within the text are provided in *Forest Stewardship Bulletins No. 4 (Terminology)* and *No. 7 (Timber Harvesting: An Essential Management Tool).*

PLANNING

Objective:

To optimize short-term and long-term benefits of forest management activities through adequate planning.

Issue:

Management activities undertaken without planning can produce undesirable environmental, economic, and aesthetic consequences.

Considerations and concerns:

1. Many private landowners are not aware of the values available from their forestland.

2. Many private landowners do not define what they want from their forestland.

3. Many private landowners do not involve resource professionals in forest management planning.

4. Forest management activities, particularly harvesting, are often undertaken for short-term gain, without thought for the forest's future.

BMPs:

1. Inventory resources on the property, including general plant-tree communities, water resources (*streams, spring seeps*—a class of wetland created by groundwater emerging in small pools surrounded by vegetation, *wetlands, vernal ponds*), soils, and unique areas (*endangered, threatened,* or *rare species* habitat, rock outcroppings, notable views).

   a. Initially inventory at a level of detail necessary to address preliminary goals and objectives.

   b. Later conduct a more detailed analysis to meet specific landowner operational needs, such as harvesting.

   c. Be aware of how the resources on the property fit in with the surrounding landscape.

2. Work with a natural resource professional to identify preliminary goals and objectives.

3. Mark and maintain property boundary lines.

4. Develop realistic goals and objectives based on the resource inventory and available landowner time and finances. Be as specific as possible when enumerating objectives (e.g., does "managing for wildlife" mean creating habitat for a wide variety of wildlife or concentrating on habitat requirements for one or two species).

5. Consider the effects of planned activities on surrounding properties.

6. Create a written management plan based on the resource inventory and landowner objectives. Include a map showing stands or management units and a timetable for completion of recommended activities.

For additional information:

Fajvan, Mary Ann. *Pennsylvania Woodlands No. 9: Developing a Woodland Management Plan.* College of Agricultural Sciences, Penn State Cooperative Extension, University Park, Pa.

Finley, James C. *Pennsylvania Woodlands No. 3: Resource Evaluation.* College of Agricultural Sciences, Penn State Cooperative Extension, University Park, Pa.

Harvey, Helene, and James C. Finley. *Forest Stewardship Bulletin No. 6: Planning Your Forest's Future.* DCNR Bureau of Forestry, Harrisburg, Pa.

Jones, Stephen B., and Roe S. Cochran. *Pennsylvania Woodlands No. 11: Managing Your Woodlot with the Help of a Consulting Forester.* College of Agricultural Sciences, Penn State Cooperative Extension, University Park, Pa.

FOREST OPERATIONS
Regeneration and Renewal

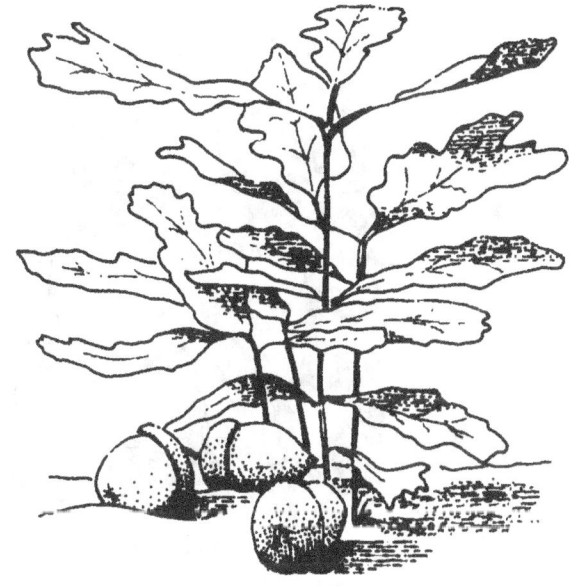

Objective:

To ensure that the forest of the future is a productive forest.

Issue:

Timber is being harvested without regard for forest regeneration and renewal (growth of a new forest plant community).

Considerations and concerns:

1. Pennsylvania's forests are maturing; harvesting should lead to renewal.

2. Preharvest assessment of advanced regeneration and potential problems will minimize the possibility of regeneration failure.

3. Deer are having a major impact on forest regeneration.

4. Pennsylvania forests lack advanced regeneration of desirable species.

5. Once seed sources of desirable species are gone, it is difficult to reproduce a productive forest for the future.

BMPs:

1. Assess advanced regeneration, seed sources for postharvest regeneration, and potential stump and root sprouting.

2. Assess and, if necessary, control competing vegetation such as ferns, grasses, and other undesirable *understory* tree and shrub species.

3. Assess and, if necessary, control the potential loss of seed, seedlings, and sprouts to deer and other wildlife.

4. Provide for regeneration each time harvests are made under the uneven-aged system.

5. Consider the biological requirements of the species you want to regenerate, whether by natural reproduction or planting.

For additional information:

Bihun, Yuri, James C. Finley, Stephen B. Jones, and Ellen Roane. *Forest Stewardship Bulletin No. 7: Timber Harvesting: An Essential Tool of Forest Stewardship.* DCNR Bureau of Forestry, Harrisburg, Pa.

Grace, James R. *Pennsylvania Woodlands No. 8: Principles of Silviculture.* College of Agricultural Sciences, Penn State Cooperative Extension, University Park, Pa.

Grace, James R. *Pennsylvania Woodlands No. 10: Hardwood Management for Economic Return.* College of Agricultural Sciences, Penn State Cooperative Extension, University Park, Pa.

FOREST OPERATIONS
Tending
Stand—residual stand protection

Objective:

To minimize the negative impacts of management activities on vegetation remaining on the site.

Issue:

The stand that will remain after intermediate treatments is subject to damage or degradation during forest management operations.

Considerations and concerns:

1. Intermediate treatments should leave the forest in better condition than it was in before the activity was undertaken.

2. Careless operation of equipment results in damaged trees.

3. Proper planning can minimize the chances of damaging or degrading the residual stand.

BMPs:

1. Focus on protection of the residual stand rather than on the trees being removed.

2. During intermediate operations, retain seed source of species needed to achieve long-term management objectives.

3. Avoid intermediate cuttings that may increase interfering plant communities, such as grasses and ferns, or be prepared to treat interfering vegetation before the regeneration cut.

4. Design and lay out *skid trails* (trails, used to drag logs, that require less construction than skid roads because of less frequent use) and *skid roads* (designed for frequent use by skidding equipment and usually incorporating water control structures) to minimize damage by avoiding residual trees and using *bumper trees* (trees left standing along skid trails and roads until the end of the harvesting operation) to protect them from skidding damage.

5. Exercise special care when harvesting trees during the growing season (usually between April and August), when residual trees are most susceptible to felling and skidding damage.

6. Identify and mark unique vegetation to be protected.

7. Ensure that a stand compatible with long-term management objectives remains after intermediate treatments. Instead of selecting for cutting, select for retention:
   a. species adapted to the site
   b. trees not likely to develop *epicormic branching* (branching that occurs after other branches have developed higher on the tree trunk) from exposure to increased sunlight
   c. properly spaced trees

8. Avoid high-grading (see page 2).

For additional information:

Grace, James R. *Pennsylvania Woodlands No. 10: Hardwood Management for Economic Return.* College of Agricultural Sciences, Penn State Cooperative Extension, University Park, Pa.

FOREST OPERATIONS
Tending
Stand—insects, diseases, and fire

Objective:
To minimize the adverse effects of insects, diseases, and fire on forest resources.

Issue:
Insects, diseases, and fire can make it difficult to accomplish forest management goals and objectives.

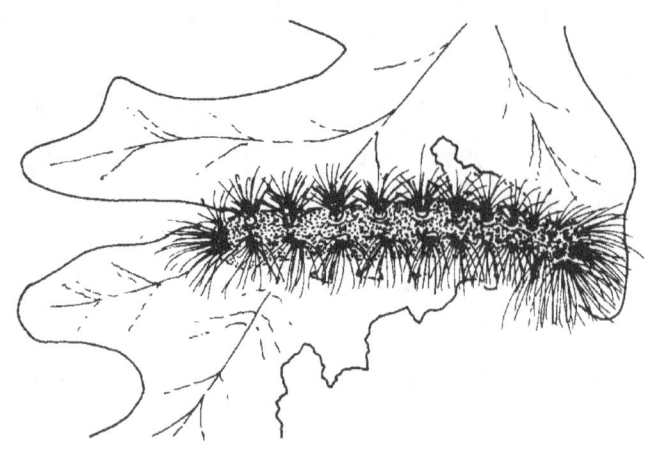

Considerations and concerns:

1. Most landowners and some resource professionals fail to recognize the effects of insects and diseases on forests.

2. Proper management can minimize the impacts of insects and diseases.

3. Landowner objectives may have to be modified to deal with insects and diseases.

BMPs:

1. Monitor insect and disease populations.

2. Take appropriate control measures when insects or diseases are likely to prevent the accomplishment of landowner goals and objectives.

3. Consider increasing species diversity, changing species composition, or changing stand structure to minimize susceptibility to insect and disease attack.

4. Maintain access roads to facilitate fire control.

5. Consider a timber harvest to salvage dead and dying trees.

For additional information:

National Acid Precipitation Assessment Program. *Diagnosing Injury to Eastern Forest Trees.* USDA Forest Service, Forest Pest Management, Atlanta, Ga., and Penn State Department of Plant Pathology, University Park, Pa.

FOREST OPERATIONS
Tending
Site quality protection—productivity

Objective:

To protect the soil's ability to sustain desired plant and animal communities.

Issue:

Operations at the wrong location and during inappropriate weather can damage soil structure and lower *site quality.*

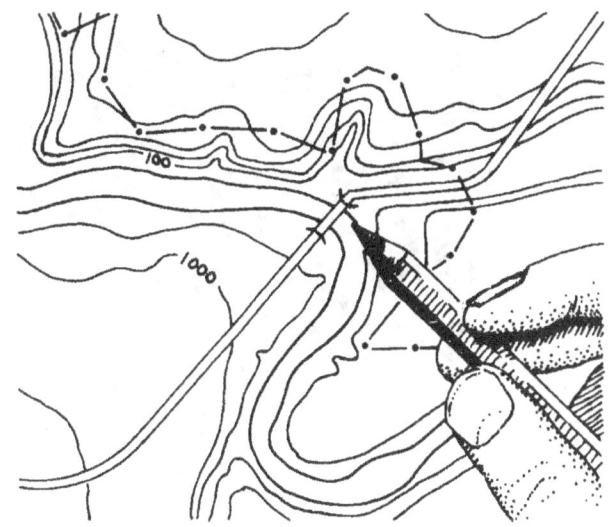

Considerations and concerns:

1. Current equipment makes it possible to move large volumes of timber in all kinds of weather and soil conditions.

2. Careful removal of forest products can be the key to having a productive forest in the future.

3. Soil compaction inhibits regeneration.

4. Deep ruts can damage roots, which can lead to decay, stain, reduced growth, and mortality.

BMPs:

1. Minimize soil compaction and rutting by matching operating techniques, season of operation, and equipment to soil types and moisture levels.

2. Use soil surveys, topographic maps, and on-site evaluations as guides when planning *log landing* (area at end of a skid road where harvested timber is stored or prepared for transport), skid road, and *haul road* (road used by trucks to move harvested timber from the log landing to its destination) locations.

3. Modify landing and road locations to reflect actual soil, *parent material* (rock from which soil is derived), and topographic conditions.

4. Keep the landing and road network at minimum size necessary to remove harvested timber efficiently.

5. Do not contaminate soils with fuels, lubricants, and other chemicals.

For additional information:

Brown, Darlene B., ed. 1993. *Best Management Practices for Silvicultural Activities in Pennsylvania's Forest Wetlands.* College of Agricultural Sciences, Penn State Cooperative Extension, University Park, Pa.

Department of Environmental Protection (DEP) Bureau of Land and Water Conservation, Cambria County Conservation District, and College of Agricultural Sciences, Penn State Cooperative Extension. *Controlling Erosion and Sedimentation from Timber Harvesting Operations.* 1992. College of Agricultural Sciences, Penn State Cooperative Extension, University Park, Pa.

FOREST OPERATIONS
Tending
Site quality protection—water resources
Objective:
To minimize the movement of soil into water resources during forest management operations.

Issue:
Erosion and sedimentation from forest management activities can affect water quality.

Considerations and concerns:
1. Operations that affect soil and water are regulated by law.
2. Small changes in the operation can eliminate many of the negative impacts.
3. Forested wetlands are often difficult to identify, especially during dry seasons.

BMPs:
1. Comply with all provisions of Chapter 102 and Chapter 105 of the Clean Streams Law and the Dam Safety and Encroachments Act, respectively.
2. Design roads to shed surface water quickly.
3. Design roads and landings to prevent or divert surface water flow.
4. Avoid locating roads and landings on *seasonly wet* soils (refers to wetlands that have water at or near the surface only during periods of abundant rainfall or snow melt).
5. Consider slope when laying out roads and landings.
6. Provide adequate riparian buffers between disturbed areas, such as roads or landings, and streams or wetlands.
7. Bridges and culverts are the preferred methods of crossing *intermittent* (not flowing continuously throughout the year) and *perennial* (continuous flow) streams. When *fords* (shallow stream sections) are used for truck crossings, stabilize the bottom with clean rock.
8. Cross wetlands only when absolutely necessary.

9. If forest operations necessitate taking heavy equipment into wetlands, conduct those operations, whenever possible, during the driest periods or when the wet area is solidly frozen.

10. Do not skid through water courses or spring seeps.

11. Do not contaminate water bodies and soil with forest management chemicals and petroleum products.

12. Retire the road network properly at the completion of operations.

For additional information:

Brown, Darlene B., ed. 1993. *Best Management Practices for Silvicultural Activities in Pennsylvania's Forest Wetlands.* College of Agricultural Sciences, Penn State Cooperative Extension, University Park, Pa.

DEP Bureau of Land and Water Conservation, Cambria County Conservation District, and College of Agricultural Sciences, Penn State Cooperative Extension. *Controlling Erosion and Sedimentation from Timber Harvesting Operations.* 1992. College of Agricultural Sciences, Penn State Cooperative Extension, University Park, Pa.

FOREST VALUES
Aesthetic Considerations

Objective:

To minimize the adverse visual effects of harvesting and other forest management activities.

Issue:

Much of the opposition to forest management activities, particularly harvesting, is due to the changed physical appearance of the area.

Considerations and concerns:

1. Most landowners are concerned about the appearance of their property.

2. Acceptance of forest management activities by the general public is increased by having the job look good.

BMPs:

1. Cut all broken trees, *leaners* (trees tipped or dislodged during a harvesting operation), and badly scarred trees except where they are being retained for a specific purpose.

2. Locate landings away from public view.

3. Protect and release from competition trees with unusual shapes and colors.

4. Design cutting areas to take advantage of natural contours; avoid straight lines when possible.

5. Lop (cut up) tops of harvested trees near public roads, frequently used trails, recreational areas, and residential sites. (Note: This might increase the adverse impacts of deer on regeneration, because intact tree tops left behind help protect young growth.)

6. Use as much of the harvested wood as possible to minimize debris. (Note: This might reduce habitat for small mammals, reptiles, amphibians, and beneficial insects.)

7. Clean up all *refuse* (man-made debris) daily.

8. Regrade and seed landings, using native grasses wherever possible.

9. Keep mud off public roads and out of streams.

10. Consider leaving a visual buffer along traveled roads.

For additional information:

Kendra, Angelina, and Ellen M. O'Donnell. *Forest Stewardship Bulletin No. 8: Planning for Beauty and Enjoyment.* DCNR Bureau of Forestry, Harrisburg, Pa.

FOREST VALUES
Understanding Wildlife Habitats

Objective:

To consider the impacts of forest management activities on wildlife resources and understand the trade-offs necessary to accomplish landowner goals and objectives.

Issue:

Forest management activities have positive and negative effects on wildlife resources.

Considerations and concerns:

1. Wildlife is important to landowners and the general public.

2. The effects of forest management activities on wildlife are often overlooked.

BMPs:

1. Inventory habitat features on the property, and be aware of their relationship to surrounding lands.

2. Protect sensitive habitats, such as spring seeps, vernal ponds, riparian zones, cliffs, caves, and *rubble land* (area with high content of large rock fragments).

3. Develop missing special habitats, such as evergreen cover, grape arbors, and herbaceous (nonwoody plants) openings, through planting, cutting, or other manipulations.

4. Protect cavity trees, snags, and food-producing shrubs and vines.

5. Maintain overhead shade along cold-water streams.

6. Use forest management activities to develop habitats required by species desired by the landowner.

For additional information:

Brooks, Robert P., Daniel A. Devlin, and Jerry Hassinger. 1994. *Wetlands and Wildlife.* College of Agricultural Sciences, Penn State Cooperative Extension, University Park, Pa.

Devlin, Daniel, and Jack Payne. *Pennsylvania Woodlands No. 6: Woodland Wildlife Management.* College of Agricultural Sciences, Penn State Cooperative Extension, University Park, Pa.

Hassinger, Jerry, Lou Hoffman, Michael J. Puglisi, Terry D. Rader, and Robert G. Wingard. 1979. *Woodlands and Wildlife.* College of Agricultural Sciences, Penn State Cooperative Extension, University Park, Pa.

Hassinger, Jerry, and Jack Payne. *Pennsylvania Woodlands No. 7: Dead Wood for Wildlife.* College of Agricultural Sciences, Penn State Cooperative Extension, University Park, Pa.

Sullivan, Kristi L., and Margaret C. Brittingham. *Forest Stewardship Bulletin No. 5: Wildlife.* DCNR Bureau of Forestry, Harrisburg, Pa.

FOREST VALUES
Species of Special Concern and Unique Habitats

Objective:

To recognize the importance and contribution of unique or special resources to the ecological integrity of the property and the Commonwealth.

Issue:

Unique areas and plant and animal species of special concern need to receive specific attention in forest management activities.

Considerations and concerns:

1. Landowners often are unaware of the existence of species of special concern or unique areas on their properties.

2. Many landowners would be willing to protect special resources on their properties if they had information and advice on what actions to take to protect them.

3. The loss of additional endangered, threatened, or rare species will diminish the biological wealth of our state.

BMPs:

1. Become aware of the presence of and protect endangered, threatened, and rare species' habitats and unique habitat features.

2. Know the habitat requirements of endangered, threatened, and rare species on the property so that activities can be planned either to avoid disturbing or to enhance these habitats.

3. Keep in mind that plant habitats can be very small and specific. Learn to recognize these special microsites (small areas in which soil nutrients, water availability, sunlight, and other resources affect only one or a few trees and other plants).

4. Develop specific management plans for unique areas and habitats with the help of a resource professional.

For additional information:

McGuinness, Barbara J., ed. 1995. *A Heritage for the 21st Century: Conserving Pennsylvania's Native Biological Diversity.* Pennsylvania Fish and Boat Commission, Harrisburg, Pa.

Pennsylvania Fish and Boat Commission and Pennsylvania Game Commission. 1985. *Endangered and Threatened Species of Pennsylvania.* Wild Resource Conservation Fund, Harrisburg, Pa.

REGULATIONS AFFECTING FOREST MANAGEMENT

Timber harvesting activities are subject to a number of federal, state, and local regulations. These include Section 404 of the Federal Water Pollution Control Act, Chapter 102 of Pennsylvania's Clean Streams Law, Chapter 105 of Pennsylvania's Dam Safety and Encroachments Act, Municipal Notification of DEP Permit Application Submittal, and Pennsylvania's Fish and Boat Code. The Pennsylvania Department of Environmental Protection can provide information about these regulations. Pennsylvania Department of Transportation (PennDOT) regulations that apply include Chapter 441, Access to and Occupancy of Highways by Driveways and Local Roads; and Chapter 189, Road Bonding Regulations.

In Pennsylvania, the Right to Practice Forestry Act and the Timber Trespass Law also apply. The DCNR Bureau of Forestry can familiarize you with these regulations, which were enacted to protect landowners and others involved with timber harvesting.

Most municipalities have regulations concerning zoning and land use. A growing number of municipalities also have regulations concerning earth moving, timber harvesting, and other activities associated with forest management. These regulations vary considerably from one municipality to another, so be sure to familiarize yourself with the laws in your area.

PENNSTATE
1855

College of Agricultural Sciences
Cooperative Extension

Visit Penn State's College of Agricultural Sciences on the Web: http://www.cas.psu.edu

Penn State College of Agricultural Sciences research, extension, and resident education programs are funded in part by Pennsylvania counties, the Commonweal h of Pennsylvania, and the U.S. Department of Agriculture.

This publication is available from the Publications Distribution Center, The Pennsylvania State University, 112 Agricultural Administration Building, University Park, PA 16802. For information telephone (814) 865-6713.

Issued in furtherance of Cooperative Extension Work, Acts of Congress May 8 and June 30, 1914, in cooperation with the U.S. Department of Agriculture and the Pennsylvania Legislature. T. R. Alter, Director of Cooperative Extension, The Pennsylvania State University.

This publication is available in alternative media on request.

The Forest Stewardship Program is administered nationally by the USDA Forest Service and is directed in Pennsylvania by the DCNR Bureau of Forestry with assistance from a statewide steering committee. The Forest Stewardship Program assists forest landowners in better managing their forestlands by providing information, education, and technical assistance. For more information about program services and publications contact: The Pennsylvania Forest Stewardship Program, DCNR Bureau of Forestry, P.O. Box 8552, Harrisburg, PA 17105-8552. Phone: (800) 235-WISE, or (717) 787-2106.

Prepared by Shelby E. Chunko, former stewardship project associate, School of Forest Resources, Penn State; and Wilbur Wolfe.

Cover Illustration by Doug Pifer. Illustrations on pages 3 thru 11 by Patrick Britten.

CAT UH102   R7.5M7/01ps4191

Pennsylvania Forest
Stewardship Program

Forests for Life

Finley, James C.; Stout, Susan L.; Pierson, Timothy G.; McGuinness, Barbara J.
2007. **Managing timber to promote sustainable forests: a second-level
course for the Sustainable Forestry Initiative of Pennsylvania.** Gen. Tech.
Rep. NRS-11. Newtown Square, PA: U.S. Department of Agriculture, Forest
Service, Northern Research Station. 47 p.

At least 80 percent of the raw material used for wood products by the forest
industry is from privately owned woodlands. This publication provides material for
a course designed to help landowners, foresters, and loggers work together to
assess whether a planned timber harvest will retain the diversity of species on site.
It includes methods for collecting overstory and understory data, inspecting these
data, and assessing sustainability.